디자이너 세종의 독창성 : 한글의 숨은 코드

Ingenious Designer Sejong : the Hidden Code in Designing Hangeul

한글의 우수성에 대해

막연한 예찬으로만 그치지 말고,

새 시선으로

한글 내부에 숨겨진 새로운 비밀을

캐내 보자.

디자이너 세종의 독창성 :
한글의 숨은 코드

Ingenious Designer Sejong :
the Hidden Code in Designing Hangeul

이 상 억

역락

책 머리에

한글의 문자 특성과 우수성을 얘기하지만 대개 막연한 예찬으로만 그칠 뿐이었으므로, 한글 창제 배경의 실제 상황 복원, 한글의 조형적 특징, 한글꼴의 발달, 한글디자인의 기본 개념과 범위 등을 꼼꼼히 따져 봐야 할 것이다. 한글 관계의 문자도(文字圖) 구성 및 세계 문자와의 비교도 해 볼 필요가 있다.

한글을 디자인하는 당시의 현장을 상상해서 실제로 백지 위에 어느 획을 어떤 식으로 그어 보았을까부터 시작해 보는 사고가 필요하다. 설사 인근 국가의 문자들을 보고 알았다 해도 거기서 일부 따와서 완성될 전체재가 아니었기에, 일사불란한 확산 논리에 의해 시초부터 끝 획까지 전체적 그림을 가지고 디자인해 나갔어야 했다.

결코 헝겊에 훈민정음 몇 장을 인쇄해 넣거나, 붓끝 솜씨로 한글을 꽃처럼 그려 썼다고 서예를 잘 한 것으로 착각해서는, 정말 한글의 디자인 과정과 구조 속의 흥미로운 비밀 코드는 전혀 이해한 것이 아니다. 처음부터 새 시선으로 한글 내부에 숨겨진 코드를 캐내 보자.

2014. 8. 12
이 상 억

Preface

There has been much talk of the characteristics and excellence of the Hangeul writing system, but in general this has been no more than vague praise of the system, so we need to give careful consideration to recreating the actual situation at the time of the creation of the writing system, as well as to the formative characteristics of Hangeul, the development of the Hangeul calligraphic styles, and the basic concepts and scope of the design of Hangeul. There is also a need to compose a pictographic map in relation to Hangeul and to compare the Korean alphabet with other writing systems around the world.

Our approach to the issue should begin with imagining the situation at the time when Hangeul was first designed, asking ourselves what strokes were made in what way on that blank sheet of paper. Even if the designers were aware of the writing systems of neighboring nations, Hangeul was a consistent system that could not have been completed by borrowing small parts of other systems, so the designers had to design Hangeul from start to finish with a complete picture in mind, following a logic of ordered expansion and addition.

We should be under no illusion that the printing of the *Hunminjeongeum* on a few scraps of paper or writing Hangeul in a flowery calligraphic style mean that the writing system was designed well; this shows a complete failure to understand the fascinating secret code hidden within the structure of the Hangeul writing system. Let us adopt a completely new perspective and unearth this code hidden within Hangeul.

2014. 8. 12   Lee Sang-Oak

차례CONTENTS

한글의 숨은 코드
570년 이상 모르고 지냈던 성은(聖恩)

새벽에 홀로 촛불을 밝히고 디자인에 몰두하고 있는 40대의 이도(李祹) 디자이너를 만난 것은 SF 속에서였다. 화선지에 묽은 먹으로 여러 방향의 획을 그어 보고 있었다. 가로 세로 직선과 사선 및 원, 점 등이 보였다. 새 문자를 구상해 보고 있다는 것이다.

그는 적어도 "낫 놓고 ㄱ자는 알게 해야 한다"는 첫 번째 화두에 잡혀 있다고 했다. 농부들이 오른손잡이가 많을 테니까 바른손으로 낫을 잡았다 놓으면 눈앞에 ㄱ이란 모양이 보이지 않느냐, 반면 그리스나 러시아[1] 사람들이 좋아하는 Γ 모양이 된다면 흔치 않은 왼손잡이 꼴이어야 하지 않느냐는 것이다. 낫을 앞에 놓고 그대로 해 보라! 어리석은 일반인까지 어여삐, 즉 불쌍

---

[1] 러시아뿐만 아니라, 불가리아의 키릴 형제가 그리스 문자의 Γ(감마)자를 따다가 키릴 문자를 만들어 퍼뜨린 슬라브 지역의 많은 문자 사용자들이 나쁜 선택의 피해를 보고 있는 것이다. 「ㄱㄴ」의 넷 중에 이도에게 ㄱ과 ㄴ이 쓰였고, 로마자에도 L, 한자에도 乚 그리고 Γ이 쓰였다.

히 여겨 이렇게 세심한 디자인의 배려까지 하고 있다는 느낌을 들게 했다.

그러나 그는 그리 단순한 디자이너만이 아니었다. 나는 적어도 70대를 들어서고 있으니, 이 40대 천재의 숨은 뜻을 읽을 수 있었다. 몇 년 안에 대단한 디자인의 산물을 터뜨릴 것이라는 예감도 느낄 수 있었다. 낫 놓고 좌우를 따지는 정도로 그를 간단히 다 이해했다고 생각하면 큰 오산이다. 그는 더 깊은 의도를 숨겨놓고 있었다.

ㄱ 대 Γ, ㄴ 대 ⌐

붓을 들고 몇 번 Γ 모양을 그려 보더니 단연 ㄱ 모양을 취해야겠다는 결심을 굳힌 듯했다. 그도 그럴 것이 Γ 모양을 그리려면 붓으로 두 획인데 ㄱ 모양은 한 획으로 가능하기 때문이다. Γ 모양을 그리고 있을 수많은 사람들이 허비하는 몇 십분의 1초씩을, ㄱ 모양을 그리는 사람들은 절약하고 있는 셈이 아닌가? 과연 디자인은 잘하면 얼마나 많은 사람들에게 득이 되고 못하면 큰 손해가 되는가를 여실히 보여주는 경우다. ㄴ의 경우도 획수 절약상 반대의 모습인 ⌐ 모양을 취하지 않았다.

ㅋ 대 F

다음에 붓을 이리저리 놀려 보더니 역시 그는 ㅋ이란 모양을 택했다. 직관적으로 ㄱ에 가획을 해서 ㅋ이란 모양을 만든 것이다. 저 별나라 서쪽에서 널리 유행하던 F라는 모양이 3획으로 써야만 한다는 딱한 사정은 몰랐지만, 좌우간 좌우가 반대인 2획의 ㅋ을 선택하여 한 천재가 또 수많은 시간을 벌어준 것이다. 감사하고 감탄할 결과다!

ㅁ 〉 ㅂ 〉 XⒽ 〉 ㅂ⌒ㅍ
cf. ㄹ/ㅌ

며칠 후 그를 다시 만나 그 사이 완성해 놓은 표를 보게 되었다. 그 중에 특히 ㅁ > ㅂ > Ⓗ으로 예상되는 가획 대신 변칙적 ㅍ을 택한 이유를 물었다. 만약 Ⓗ을 택한다면 가뜩이나 ㅁ이 한자의 '입, 구'자에서 따 왔다는 말을 들을 텐데 또 한 자를 더 모방했다 할 것이 아니냐고 웃었다. 그러나 '중국에 달라야' 한다는 웃음 뒤에는 더 심오한 배려가 또 숨어 있었다. Ⓗ을 택했다면, 달리 만들어 놓은 ㄹ이나 ㅌ과 얼핏 모양이 비슷해서 작게 썼을 때 구별하기가 쉽지 않겠다는 염려라 한다.

느닷없이 작게 쓴다니 무슨 얘기냐고 물었다. 그는 머리 속 구상에 이 글자들을 함께 써서 한 음절을 한 덩이로 네모 속에 나타내면, 읽을 때 아주 편할 것이란 예상까지 하고 있었다. 과연 줄이어 늘어놓은 ㄹㅡㄹ보다는 를이 한 눈길에 들어오는 장점이 바로 보였다. 그러나 낱자들이 작은 네모 공간 속에 축소돼 복잡해 보이는 단점도 동시에 있었다.

그는 이미 를, 틀과 같은 글자를 써 놓고 비교해 보고 있었다.

를, 틀 같은 경우가 너무 비슷해 보여 고민스럽다는 것이다. 여기에다 또 제 3의 비슷한 모양를 더하는 것(가령 루:투:무)보다는 아주 달리 플 또는 푸란 모양이 되도록 하는 편이 그나마 덜 복잡해진다는 것이다. 아, 피에 그런 깊은 뜻이!

더욱이 (ㄱ>ㅋ>) ㅋ을 써서 ㄹ이나 ㅌ과 얼핏 모양이 비슷해져서 더 큰 혼동이 올까 봐 ㆁ을 도입하였다. 그리고 ㄱ이나 ㅋ과 이렇게 모양이 다른 ㆁ이 도입된 것은 어두에서 묵음인 /ng/음의 특징을 어느 정도 나타내기 위한 것은 아니었던가 싶다.

이도 디자이너 자신도 몰랐겠지만, ㅂ 대신 ㅍ을 택한 것은 다음과 같은 결과에도 이르게 한다. 우선 ㄱ부터 ㅂ까지를 한 개의 네모 속에 가지런히 채워 넣을 수가 있을 것이다. 예상치 않던 규격 속에 자음의 조형성을 입증하였다.

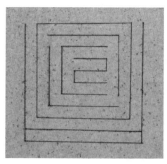

'ㄱ-ㅂ' 왼편은 석판, 오른편은 도기판

다음은 ㅋ, ㅌ, ㅍ을 더 포함시켜 ㄱ부터 ㅍ까지를 더 큰 네모 속에 가지런히 채워 넣을 수가 있을 것이다. ㅂ이라면 넣기 어려운 것을 ㅍ 모양을 택했기에 그 안에 다 그려 넣어 볼 수 있는

것이다. 이도도 몰랐을 듯한 숨은 디자인의 정체성은 수직 수평
선의 일사불란한 조합에서 이미 잉태된 것이다. 네모 규격 속에
가지런히 글자들의 조형성을 입증하였다.

'ㄱ-ㅂ, ㅌ-ㅍ'

나머지 ㅅ, ㅇ, ㅈ, ㅊ, ㅎ도 다음의 한 형상에 다 집약해 넣을
수 있다.

'ㅅ-ㅊ, ㅎ'

이 형상은 다시 다음 단계의 비밀을 열 수 있는 열쇠 구멍이었던 것이다. 이 형상[뒤에 한글, 아니 훈민정음으로 명명]에 감춰져 있는 '코드'를 읽어 가는 과정은 흥미진진할 따름이다.

그 열쇠 이야기는 잠시 묻어 두고 이도의 용의주도한 디자인 과정을 다시 돌아보자. 이도는 ㄷ을 택할 때 ㄷ ㄱㄴ라는 네 방향을 알고 있었을 것이다.2) 그 중에 ㄴ에서 가획으로 ㄷ을 취한 방향으로 밀고 나가고, 나머지 유사한 ㄱㄴㄴ는 더 취하지 않고 버렸다. 유사성을 줄여 최대한 구별이 쉽도록 하려는 배려라 할 수 있다. 더구나 오른쪽이 터진 것을 취해 놓음으로써 앞으로 ㅓ, ㅕ 같이 왼쪽으로 뿔이 난 모양과 붙여 쓸 때, ㄷ의 안쪽의 공간 침투를 허용할 수 있게 한 것이다.

이도는 이제까지 모양들을 '자음'이라 이름 짓고, 이에 합쳐 쓰일 점 ·, 수평선 ㅡ, 수직선 ㅣ를 기본으로 소위 '모음'을 만들었다. 이 ·, ㅡ, ㅣ 모양은 각각 한자에도 같은 모습이 나타난다. 대부분의 문자를 만들 때 흔히 "수직선, 수평선, 사선, 원" 등의 획을 사용하여 결합시킬 수밖에 없는 원천적인 제약이 있기 때문에 필연적 내지 체계적 일치를 보이는 유사성이 생겨 서로 비슷해지는 것이다.(이상억(1997), Graphical Ingenuity in the Korean Writing System : With New Reference to Calligraphy. In Young-Key

---

2) 아주 오랜 세월이 흐른 뒤 1927년 박용만 편찬 <됴션말 독본 첫 책>과 <됴션말 교과서 둘재 책>에 그는 영문의 d, 일문의 ㄍ, ㄴ는 영문의 v, 러시아문자의 нь를 표기하기 위한 문자로 도입했다. 외래어 표기를 위해 보조적 문자를 설정한 것이다.(홍윤표(2013) 한글이야기, 1 한글의 역사, p.296) 또 한자 중에 匚, ㄴㅣ의 형태가 있고 로마자에는 U가 있으나 이는 ㄴㅣ보다 V에서 변형된 것이다. ㄴㅣ, ㄴ은 타밀어에도 있다. 은코에도 ㄱ, ㄴㅣ이 있다.

Kim-Renaud ed., The Korean Alphabet : Its History and Structure., Honolulu : University of Hawaii Press. 107-116. 이상억(2002), 「훈민정음의 자소적(字素的) 독창성」, 고영근 외, 『문법과 텍스트』, 서울대 출판부. [이상억 1997의 국역]).

원래 ㅣ+ㆍ, ㆍ+ㅣ, ㆍ+ㅡ, ㅡ+ㆍ 조합이 ㅏㅓㅗㅜ의 결합으로 발전되었고 여기서 다시 ㅏㅑㅓㅕ, ㅗㅛㅜㅠ, ㅐㅔㅒㅖ, ㅘㅝㅙㅞ, ㅢㅚㅟ 등으로 확산된 것이다. 이 과정을 하나씩 다시 보이면 다음과 같다.

ㅗ

ㅏ   ㅓ

ㅜ

여기서 중앙에 수렴된 ㅓ 모양을 놓고 보면 모든 모음 형태가 ㅓ에서 추출된 것임을 알 수 있다.

ㅗ

ㅏ   ╋   ㅓ

ㅜ

여기에 우선 한 둘레씩 확산된 글자를 더해 보자.

ㅛ
ㅗ

ㅏ ㅑ   ╫   ㅓ ㅕ

ㅜ
ㅠ

수렴형은 ㅒ이다. 다음에 ㅔ, ㅐ와 ㅘ, ㅝ가 더해진다.

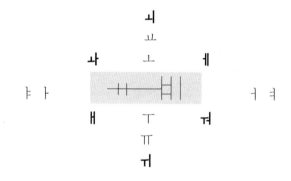

그리고 ㅚ, ㅟ 두 글자가 도입된다. <내부의 **열쇠** 모양 도형에서 모든 모음자형을 만들어 낼 수 있다. 차례대로 획을 구성해 보면 마치 열쇠와 같은 모습 속에서 모든 가능성이 나온다.>

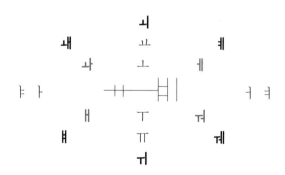

마지막 단계로 ㅒ, ㅖ, ㅙ, ㅞ 네 글자가 추가된다.

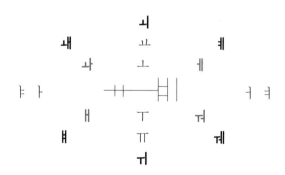

한편 ·, ㅡ,ㅣ 즉, 모음의 기본 도형 ·(天 하늘), ㅡ(地 땅), ㅣ(人 사람)에서 ㅓ를 생성한다. 이상으로 현재 한글에서 쓰이는 21개 모음이 다 나타났지만, 원래는 .ㅣ도 있었으나 현재는 쓰이지 않는다.

1) ㅏ ㅓ   ㅗ ㅜ
2) ㅏ ㅑ ㅓ ㅕ   ㅗ ㅛ ㅜ ㅠ
3) ㅏ ㅑ ㅓ ㅕ   ㅗ ㅛ ㅜ ㅠ   ㅐ   ㅔ   ㅘ   ㅝ
4) ㅏ ㅑ ㅓ ㅕ   ㅗ ㅛ ㅜ ㅠ   ㅐ   ㅔ   ㅘ   ㅝ
                                              ㅚ   ㅟ
5) ㅏ ㅑ ㅓ ㅕ   ㅗ ㅛ ㅜ ㅠ   ㅐ ㅒ ㅔ ㅖ ㅘ ㅙ ㅝ ㅞ
                                              ㅚ ㅢ ㅟ

여기 위 8개 모음 속에 열쇠 모습이 있었다. 앞서 보인 다음과 같은 자음 도형의 원, 즉 열쇠 구멍 속에다 위 **열쇠**를 넣는다고 상상해 보라. 물론 이것이 이도가 의도한 것이라고까지 말하기는 어렵다. 다만 이런 흥미로운 도형상의 맞춤이 가능할 수 있다는 비밀을 찾아보자는 것일 뿐이다. 한글 도형에 숨어 있던 흥미로운 자·모음관계를 이런 식으로 디자인상의 숨은 코드로 엿볼 수 있다 하겠다. 마치 숨어있던 열쇠를 찾아 열쇠 구멍에 넣고 새로운 시야의 문을 연다는 상징성이 있다.

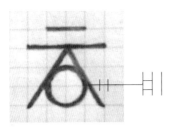

이도의 머리 속 구상에 이 글자들을 함께 써서 한 음절을 한 덩이로 네모 속에 나타내면, 읽을 때 아주 편할 것이란 예상을 하고 있었다는 얘기를 다시 해보며 SF를 끝내자.

중성이 ㅏ, ㅐ, ㅑ, ㅒ, ㅓ, ㅔ, ㅕ, ㅖ, ㅣ일 때는 중성을 초성의 오른쪽에 붙여 쓴다. 종성이 있으면 그 아래 붙여 쓴다. ∞:ㅣ

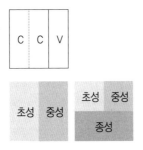

중성이 ㅗ, ㅛ, ㅜ, ㅠ, ㅡ일 때는 중성을 아래쪽에 붙여 쓴다. 종성은 그 아래 붙여 쓴다. 훍, 듧

		C			
C		V		C	
C	C		C	C	C

중성이 ㅘ, ㅙ, ㅚ, ㅝ, ㅞ, ㅟ, ㅢ와 같이 아래쪽에 붙이는 모음과 오른쪽에 붙이는 모음의 복합일 때는 다음과 같이 아래쪽에 먼저, 그 다음 오른쪽에 붙여 쓴다. 종성은 마찬가지로 아래쪽에 붙여 쓴다. 빗, 활

이 음절 단위 네모 구성 방식은 한자에서 江, 部, 忠, 碧 등의 구성에서 변, 방, 받침 등이 그 위치를 보여준 선례가 있다.

✜ 참고

한글 자형과 관련이 있는 넓은 범위의 폰트들

· ‒ ㅣ ㅣ I Ⅰ ㅏ ㅓ ㅗ ㅜ ㅏ ㅓ ㅗ ㅜ ㅑ ㅕ ㅕ ㅓ ㅗ ㅛ ㅠ ㅜ ㅠ Ⅰ.ⅠН ㅐ ㅔ ㅒ ㅖ
±土王
「 ㄱ」 ㄴ ㄴ ㄱ ㄱ ㄴ ㄴ ㄱ」 ㄱ ㄷ ㄹ ㄱ ㄲ ㄴ ㄴ
ㄷ ㄸ ㄱ ㄱ ㄲ ㅁ ㅂ ㅃ ㄷ ㄷ ㅁ F ㅌ ㅌ ㅋ ㅋ ㅃ ㄷ ㅃ ㄹ ㅇ ㅇ ㅂ ㅂ ㅂ ㄱ ㅣ ㅍ ㅍ ㅌ
／ ／ ＼ ＼ ／ ＼ ＼ ＼ ＼ Λ Ｖ ＜＞ ＜＞∠ ∠ ∠ ∠ ∠ ∠ ∠ ∠ ∠ ∠ ∠ ∠ ㅈ ㅊ ㅊ ㅅ
KΣ ㅆ MWNИZ≤≥×X
▽ ◁▷ ◁◁ △ ▲ ▽ A A ◇ ○ O ㅎ

훈민정음의 자소적(字素的) 독창성
서예의 관점에서

훈민정음에는 (1) 가획 (2) 합자 두 가지 특징 외에, 다음과 같은 서예상의 원칙들이 적용되었다고 볼 수 있다. (3) 왼쪽에서 오른쪽으로 또 위에서 아래로 쓴다. (4) 가획을 할 때와 음절 단위 내부를 합자해 써나갈 때 같은 간격을 유지한다. (5) 음절 단위의 크기를 네모의 연쇄로 붙여나갈 때 같은 크기를 유지한다. (6) 획수의 최소화, 즉 서예의 경제에 관한 흥미로운 또 한 예는 원래의 ∧에서 후에 ㅅ과 〈 같은 모습으로 발전된 것이다. ㄱ, ㅋ, ㄴ의 경우, 세종이 반대의 모습인 Γ, F, ⌐ 을 선택하지 않은 이유도 후자가 붓글씨로 쓸 때 한 획씩 더 요구되기 때문이다. (7) 서예적 유사성이 많을 경우 다른 자형을 도입하여 회피하도록 선택했다. (8) 자소의 최대 변별 원칙을 지키려면 ㅋ 또는 ㄴ 과 ㄷ 또는 ⊐중 하나가 선택되어야 했다. 모음자 창제시의 수직/수평선의 분포에 대한 계량적 고찰을 하면, 현재와 같은 선택이 모음자 출현 빈도에 비추어 현명한 선택이었다. 또 'ㅑ'와 'ㅕ'는 가능한 조합이며 중세국어에서도 필요한 글자였을 듯하지만, 세종이 제안하지는 않았다. 그러나 현대 방언음에서 '돴다'라든가 축약형으로 '바꼈다'를 표기할 필요성이 있다.

1. 들어가기

훈민정음과 그 창제 당시 관련성이 있었을 듯한 타문자 체계 간에 몇 글자라도 (우연 내지 비체계적) 일치관계를 세워 보려는 노력이 끊임없이 있기는 했지만, 여전히 필연적 내지 체계적 일치를 보이는 선행 문자는 딱히 알려진 바 없다. 간혹 그럴듯한 유사성이 생긴 이유는 대부분의 문자를 만들 때 흔히 "수직선, 수평선, 사선, 원" 등의 획을 사용하여 결합시킬 수밖에 없는 원천적인 제약이 있기 때문이다. Ledyard(1966)과 유창균(1966)은 팏바 문자가 훈민정음의 모델이었을 가능성이 있다고 했다. 사실 팏바 ꡊ[d]와 ꡙ[l]은 훈민정음의 ㄷ[t]과 ㄹ[l]과 자형의 일부분이 비슷하다. 그러나 다른 자들의 경우 팏바 ㄹ[ŋ], ㅅ[o], ㅈ[o], ㅌ[j]은 전혀 훈민정음 **ㄹ**, **ㅅ**, **ㅈ**, **ㅌ**과 같은 음가를 가지고 있지 않다. 이 정도의 우연한 유사성만 가지고는 아무도 양자 간에 체계적 대응이 있다고 주장할 수가 없다. 근간 제기된 각필(角筆) 기원설도 이 범주를 벗어나지는 못한다. 약간 센세이셔널한 어조로 주장하다보니 자형의 기하학적 원천제약상 유사성을 마치 '부호자 기원설'이라고 하였으나, 음가의 일치가 없어 곤란

하다. 결국 또 하나의 가설을 내놓은 것이다.

'훈민정음'이란 책 속에 자음자는 여러 음성기관의 모양을 본
떴다고 명시했고, 모음자는 천(天), 지(地), 인(人) 삼재(三才)를 기본
으로 창제하였다 했다. 이 명백한 표명은 그 앞선 어떤 문자나
도형에서 훈민정음의 뼈대를 엮어 왔다 한들, 음성기관 상형설
로 ㄱ, ㄴ 등을 설명해 나간 탁견을 퇴색시키지는 못할 것이다.
모음자 제정에 대해서 삼재를 기본으로 했다는 철학적 해석도
여전히 독창적 설명이다. 그 점과 획들이 각필의 점토(點吐) 모양
과 유사할 뿐 조사, 어미에 해당하는 역할을 가진 것이 아니라면
결코 발상의 궤가 같지 않은 것이다.

훈민정음의 두 가지 특징은 (1) 기본자에 가획(加劃)에 의해 글
자를 더 만들어 내는 것 (2) 한자 벽(甓)자처럼 최대 세 부분으로
구성된 공간에 두 자 이상을 채워 넣어(合字하여) 한 음절 단위를
이룬다는 것이다. 이 두 가지 특징 외에 다음과 같은 서예(또는
서법)상의 원칙들이 적용되었다고 볼 수 있다. 즉 (3) 왼쪽에서
오른쪽으로 또 위에서 아래로 쓴다. (4) 가획을 할 때와 음절 단
위 내부를 합자해 써 나갈 때 같은 간격을 유지한다. (5) 음절
단위의 크기를 네모의 연쇄로 붙여 나갈 때 같은 크기를 유지한
다. 이 모든 원칙들은 대칭과 안정감을 주는 것이다.

빼   니   를   그   꿱

수평으로 조밀   수평으로 소략   수직으로 조밀   수직으로 소략   가장 조밀

〈그림 1〉

앞에서 보였듯이 획들을 평행으로 써나갈 경우 여러 단계의 밀도가 있다. 수평 방향으로 여섯 겹의 획, 수직 방향으로 일곱 겹의 획이 쓰이는 경우가 가장 복잡한 단계로 보인다.

2. 훈민정음의 자소(字素)들은 어떻게 고안되었을까?

이제부터 훈민정음의 자소와 서예적 양상에 대해 과거에 연구되지 않았던 면을 살펴보기로 한다. 첫째로 아직 질의된 일이 없는 질문으로서, 세종대왕은 여러 가능한 획과 글자 모양을 백지 위에 어떻게 실험하며 창제했을까 하는 의문이다. 비록 세자들과 궁중학자들 일부가 이 계획의 각기 다른 단계에서 도왔을 수도 있겠으나, 대왕 자신이 모든 아이디어의 발안자라고 가정하는 것이 옳겠다. 왜냐 하면 이 계획이 여럿의 의견수렴(brainstorming)을 거쳐 단초가 시작되었다기보다는 애초에 한 개인이 아이디어를 배태했었다고 보아야 자연스럽기 때문이다. 이기문(1997)도 같은 시기에 같은 생각을 발표하였다.

(원래 이 생각과 본고는 1992년 8월 조지 워싱턴대에서 개최되었던 국제한국언어학회(ICKL)에서 동시에 발표되었었고 5년 후 하와이대출판부에서 영문으로 출간되었다. 영문 원고는 책 뒤쪽에 싣는다.)

〈표 1〉 중세국어의 23초성자음(오른쪽)과 중세중국어의 36성모(왼쪽)

조음방식 / 조음위치	전청 (全淸)	차청 (次淸)	전탁 (全濁)	불청불탁 (不淸不濁)
아음(牙音)	見 } 君 ㄱ	溪 } 快 ㅋ	群 } 虯 ㄲ	疑 } 業 ㆁ
설음(舌音)	端 知 } 斗 ㄷ	透 徹 } 呑 ㅌ	定 澄 } 覃 ㄸ	泥 娘 } 那 ㄴ
순음(脣音)	幫 非 } 彆 ㅂ	滂 敷 } 漂 ㅍ	竝 奉 } 步 ㅃ	明 微 } 彌 ㅁ
치음(齒音)	精 照 } 卽 ㅈ 心 審 } 戌 ㅅ	淸 穿 } 侵 ㅊ	從 牀 } 慈 ㅉ 邪 禪 } 邪 ㅆ	
후음(喉音)	影 } 挹 ㆆ	曉 } 虛 ㅎ	匣 } 洪 ㆅ	喩 } 欲 ㅇ
반설음(半舌音)				來 } 閭 ㄹ
반치음(半齒音)				日 } 穰 ㅿ

  주지하듯이 중국 운서에는 <표 1>과 같이 36 성모(聲母)가 쓰였으나 훈민정음에서는 23개만이 쓰였다. 세종은 중국 운학을 잘 알았기 때문에 그를 참조하여 국어 음운 체계를 분석하기 시작하였을 것이고 그 결과 <표 1>에 보였듯이 23개로 통합 정리하였을 것이다. 이러한 창제 준비과정에서 세종은 일종의 '시행착오' 방법을 썼을 것이고, 결코 그 신하들이 칭송했듯이 모든 글자의 전체 모습에 대한 성숙한 아이디어를 일시에 신비스러운 영감으로 얻은 것은 아닐 것이다. 이런 추론의 근거로 모음에 [천(天)의 상징으로] 둥근 점이 쓰이다가 이 모양이 비실용적으로 밝혀지자 짧은 획으로 후에 대체된 예가 있다(ㆍ > ㅗ). 세종은 훈민정음이 일반에 공개된 후에도 그 공식적 최종안을 개정, 개선하는 데 인색하지 않았던 것이다.

  또 하나 의미 있는 개정은 자형이 원래 '석보상절'에서는 직선과 직각으로 되어 붓으로 쓰기 어려운 모양이었으나 후기의 '월인석보'에서는 붓글씨에 맞도록 수정된 것이다. 세종은 아마 훈민정음의 초고를 쓸 때 붓을 사용하였을 것이고 둥근 점과 각진 획을 그리기가 어렵다는 점을 이내 느꼈을 것이다(후기 참조).

2.1. 서예(획수)의 경제

ㄱ, ㅋ, ㄴ의 경우, 세종이 반대의 모습인 Γ, F, ⅃을 선택하지 않은 이유는 후자가 붓글씨로 쓸 때 한 획씩 더 요구되기 때문이다. 이런 경우를 토대로 또 하나의 서예상 원칙을 세울 수 있다. 즉 (6) 획수의 최소화이다. 서예의 경제에 관한 흥미로운 또 한 예는 원래의 ㅅ, ㅈ, ㅊ에서 후에 ㅅ, ㅈ, ㅊ이나 〈, ㇋, ㇌과 비슷한 모습으로 발전된 것이다. 획수가 2, 3, 4에서 1, 1, 2로 크게 줄어든 것이다.

2.2. 서예적 유사성의 회피

세종이 자음자를 창제할 때, 아마 몇 가지 비슷한 글자를 <그림 2>의 점선 내 부분처럼 그려 보았을 수 있다. 이 중 ㅌ과 ㄹ은 오늘날에도 작은 활자로 인쇄되었을 경우 흔히 혼동된다. 나머지 ㅋ와 ㅂ은 선택되지 않았다. 그 까닭은 (7) 서예적 유사성이 많을 경우 다른 자형을 도입하여 회피하도록 선택했다.

세종은 ㅋ를 선택하지 않음으로 자소적 충돌을 피하면서, ㄱ

과 ㅋ을 다른 소리들보다 한 칸씩 내려놓고 맨 위에 ㆁ을 특례적으로 도입하였다. (ㆁ은 ㅇ 위에 ㅊ의 꼭지 ' 과 같은 것을 붙여 만들었을 것이다.)

세종은 ㆁ이 ㅇ과 비슷하다고 생각했는데 중국 운서에서부터 이 두 소리는 혼동되고 있었기 때문이다. 강신항(1990)에 의하면 과거 중국어에는 [ŋ]에 대해 한 글자 그리고 [ɦ] 또는 [j]에 대해 또 한 글자가 있었다 한다. 원나라 이후 [ŋ]이 사라지고 [ɦ] 또는 [j]에 합류되었으나, 세종은 중국 운학에 밝았으므로 [ŋ]과 [ɦ] 또는 [j]에 각각 대응되도록 ㆁ과 ㅇ을 따로 창제하였던 것이다. 그는 의도적으로 두 글자에 원이라는 공통의 모양을 주기 위해 ㄱ에서 ㅋ으로 이어지는 (그리고 ㅋ까지 가야 할) 규칙성을 위반한 것이었다.

김완진(1975)은 중국 운서에 근거하여 ㆁ과 ㅇ 간의 일반적 혼동을 교정해 보려 했던 세종의 무리한 시도를 비판했다. 그러나 필자는 ㅇ의 도입은 자소적 충돌(점선 내 부분처럼 ㅋ이 필요하게 되면 결과적으로 ㅋ, ㅌ, ㄹ 등의 비슷한 글자들이 많아져 혼동이 심해졌을 것임)을 피하기 위한 조치로 높이 평가하는 것이 훈민정음의 다른 독창적 면과도 조화되는 비평이라고 믿는다.

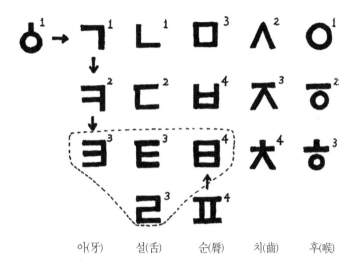

아(牙)　　　설(舌)　　　순(脣)　　　치(齒)　　　후(喉)

〈그림 2〉 훈민정음 창제 과정의 상상적 도안 원고

(어깨 숫자는 획수, 점선 내 부분처럼 ㅋ, ㅌ이 도입되면 결국 ㅋ, ㅌ, ㅌ, ㄹ 등의 비슷한 글자들이 많아져 혼동이 심해졌을 것이라 ㆁ과 ㅍ이 각각 ㅋ과 ㅌ에 대체되어 들어옴.)

　　그러나 ㆁ과 ㅇ에 의해 표기된 소리의 유사성을 말하면서도 ㆁ과 ㅇ에 분명히 각기 다른 음가를 배당한 것은 역설적이다. 더군다나 세종이 훈민정음 제자해에서 혀뿌리로 목구멍을 막는 소리로 [ŋ]을 기술한 것은 잘못된 것인데, [ŋ]은 목구멍은 열고 '연구개'를 막는 소리인 것이다. 그가 당시에 입안 뒤쪽의 움직임을 명확히 관찰할 수 없었을 터이니 '연구개'를 목구멍으로 잘못 인식한 것은 이해할 만하다. 세종이 아무리 당대의 뛰어난 음성학자였다지만 내시경 같은 기구로 실험할 수는 없었을 것이다.

　　비록 필자는 팍바 문자와 훈민정음의 관계에 대한 가정을 부인했지만, 굳이 유사점을 찾자면 ㄸ에서 바깥 부분이 ㄱ자로 그리고 안에 남은 모양이 ㅇ으로 발전된 것이라 할 만하다. 그러나 ㅁ은 기본적으로 순음이며 ㅇ은 목구멍을 상징한 자음이므로, 위와 같은 추론은 서로 섞일 수 없는 두 가지 다른 모양을 대상으로 한 가정일 뿐이다.

김완진(1975)에 의하면, 많은 학자들이 ㅁ 위에 '두' 추가획이 붙어 ㅂ이 된 것이라고 믿고 있다 하나, 필자는 그렇게 믿으면 안 된다고 본다. ㅁ은 3획인데 ㅂ도 4획이면 쓸 수 있으니 사실은 한 획만 더 추가된 것임을 알아야 한다.

ㅂ에 관해, 이 모양은 한자(漢字) 日과 혹사하며 또 ㅌ이나 (추론상의) ㅋ과도 흡사하다. 그러므로 <그림 2>에서 충돌회피를 위해 ㅐ를 90도 돌려 ㅍ을 도입한 듯하다. ㅁ이 ㅂ으로 가획된 뒤 日로까지 가야 하겠지만 점선 내의 4개 모양이 너무 비슷하여 日과 같이 4획인 ㅍ으로 대체한 셈이다. ㅐ처럼 세우는 모양이 더 자연스런 가획의 모습이지만 모음 ㅐ 앞에 붙여 ㅐㅐ같은 모양을 만들 때나 (가령 퓨 대신) 같은 모양을 이룰 때는 문제가 있다.

2.3. 자소(字素)의 최대 변별

마지막이지만 경시할 수 없는 경우로, ㄱ에 가획하여 ㄱ이란 모양을 취하지 않고 ㅋ을 선택한 이유가 ㄷ이란 모양과 혼동될 가능성을 미리 회피한 것이 아닌가 싶다. 이와 비슷하게 ㄴ에 가획하면 ㄴ이란 모양도 가능하다. (8) 자소의 최대 변별 원칙을 지키면서 ㅋ 또는 ㄴ과 ㄷ 또는 ㄱ 중 하나가 선택되어야 했다. 최대 변별력은 서예적 유사성의 회피와 함께 서예적 원칙의 제 항목들이 될 것이다.(p.14. '공간 침투'도 참고)

사실 서예에 관심을 두고 디자인 면에서 한글을 성찰해 한글 디자인의 심층에 묻혀있는 비밀스러운 면모를 캐내는 것이 꼭 필요하다. 이 책의 첫째 글은 그런 관점에서 본 결과 얻은 해석 인데, 안상수 서체나 이상봉 패션 등의 표면적 디자인에는 주목 하면서, 문자론의 넓은 안목을 가지고 더 정통적으로 한글 디자 인을 분석하는 해석을 받아들이지 않는다면 세종대왕께 송구스 러운 일이다.

3. 현재의 모음 모양을 취한 덕에 얼마나 편한가?

이상억(1997)에서는 훈민정음 모음자 창제시의 수직/수평선의 분포와 선택에 대한 계량적 고찰이 있었다. 현재와 같은 선택이 모음자 출현 빈도에 비추어 현명한 선택이었는데 이 사실을 세 종이 그 당대에 알고 한 것인지 흥미롭다. 세종은 주로 본인이 주도하여 자형 선택을 했을 텐데, [a, ja, ə, jə, i] 모음은 수직선, [o, jo, u, ju, ɨ] 모음은 수평선을 배당하였다. 이런 배당의 이유 는 아마도 먼저 보인 모음들이 더 자주 쓰이는 것들이므로(<표 2> 참조), 긴 수직선의 획이 붓으로 내리쓸 때 수직의 축을 이루 며 운필상 편리하기에 배당했다고 볼 수 있다.

아래의 <표 2>는 정인상(15세기), 김흥규(16~19세기), 유재원(20세기) 교수들이 조사한 3가지 다른 출현 빈도의 미공간 자료들과 또 유재원(1985)를 병렬한 것이다. 처음 두 난은 15세기의 고유어와 한자어 각각에서의 자모 빈도 조사로 주참조 대상이며, 셋째 난은 16~19세기 자료, 넷째 난은 20세기의 고유어만의 조사로 보조적 참조 대상이다.

〈표 2〉 다른 세 시기의 모음자의 빈도

	15C.고유어 자료		15C.한자어 자료		Cf. 16~19C. 자료		20C.고유어	
A. 수직축의 모음자								
ㅏ a	4532	14.14%	6252	15.33%	85555	19.93%	28580	24.23%
ㅐ ɛ	922	2.88%	1291	3.17%	7777	1.81%	6171	5.23%
ㅑ ja	548	1.71%	674	1.65%	6957	1.62%	828	0.70%
ㅒ jɛ	26	0.08%	26	0.06%	10	0.002	11	0.009
ㅓ ə	1803	5.62%	2935	7.20%	31995	7.45%	15652	13.27%
ㅔ e	694	2.16%	929	2.28%	11819	2.75%	2208	1.87%
ㅕ jə	1184	3.69%	1817	4.46%	33743	7.86%	2466	2.09%
ㅖ je	359	1.12%	426	1.04%	3825	0.89%	185	0.16%
ㅣ I	7043	21.97%	8200	20.11%	63103	14.70%	21785	18.47%
ㆎ ʌi	730	2.28%	730	1.79%	10762	2.51%	—	—
소 계		55.65%		57.09%		59.52%		66.03%
B. 수평축의 모음자								
ㅜ u	3612	11.27%	4669	11.45%	53392	12.44%	11413	9.68%
ㅗ o	221	0.69%	368	0.90%	5696	1.33%	314	0.27%
ㅛ jo	1015	3.17%	2096	5.14%	31251	7.28%	14189	12.03%
ㅠ ju	77	0.24%	186	0.46%	6957	1.62%	155	0.13%
ㅡ ɨ	2520	7.86%	2806	6.88%	33795	7.87%	10299	8.73%
ㆍ ʌ	5582	17.41%	5585	13.70%	18064	4.21%	—	—
소 계		40.64%		38.53%		34.75%		30.84%

	15C.고유어 자료		15C.한자어 자료		Cf. 16~19C. 자료		20C.고유어	
C. 양축의 모음자								
ㅘ wa	302	0.94%	567	1.39%	7889	1.84%	718	0.61%
ㅙ wɛ	45	0.14%	51	0.13%	231	0.05%	200	0.17%
ㅚ ∅	274	0.85%	340	0.83%	2946	0.69%	899	0.76%
ㅓ wə	56	0.17%	131	0.32%	3092	0.72%	246	0.21%
ㅔ we	6	0.02%	6	0.01%	86	0.02%	74	0.06%
ㅟ y	154	0.48%	272	0.67%	2993	0.70%	1304	1.11%
ㅢ ii	355	1.11%	422	1.03%	7359	1.71%	233	0.20%
소 계		3.71%		4.38%		5.78%		3.13%
총 계	100%		100%		100%		100%	

<표 2>에서 볼 수 있듯이 수직축 모음자 A 무리는 수평축 모음자 B보다 더 높은 빈도이므로, 만약 모양을 뒤바꾸었더라면 (예 : ㅏ를 [o]음에, ㅗ를 [a]음에 등등) 서예 운필상 아주 비효율적이고 어색한 결과가 되었을 것이다.

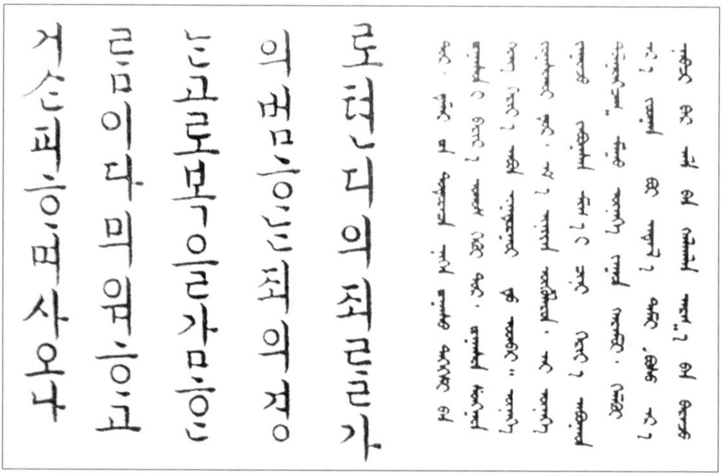

〈그림 3〉 궁체(왼쪽)와 몽골 서체

<그림 3>에 보듯이 소위 '궁체'와 몽골 서체 양자에 다같이 명백한 수직축이 나타난다. 이런 종류의 서체에서는 수직획에 가장 자주 쓰이는 소리를 배당하는 것이 바람직하다. 즉 국어의 경우에는 모음에 대해 이를 적용하면 좋겠다(몽골서체에서는 자·모음이 모두 수직축에 따라 쓰이므로 선택할 필요가 없다).

세종이 음운의 빈도와 수직획의 배당 사이에 관계를 시켰든 아니든, 현재 모습의 모음자형을 구성한 덕에 서예가로부터 일반인까지 많은 편의를 얻어 온 셈이다. 그러나 요즘에는 반대의 선택(고빈도 모음에 수평획을 배당함)이 더 편리하지 않을까 하는 생각을 하게도 된다. 대부분의 사람이 요즘에는 수평적으로 쓰기 때문이다. 하지만 여전히 붓이 아닌 펜으로 쓰는 현대에도 훈민정음에서의 선택이 실용적이라고 할 수 있다(<그림 4> 참조).

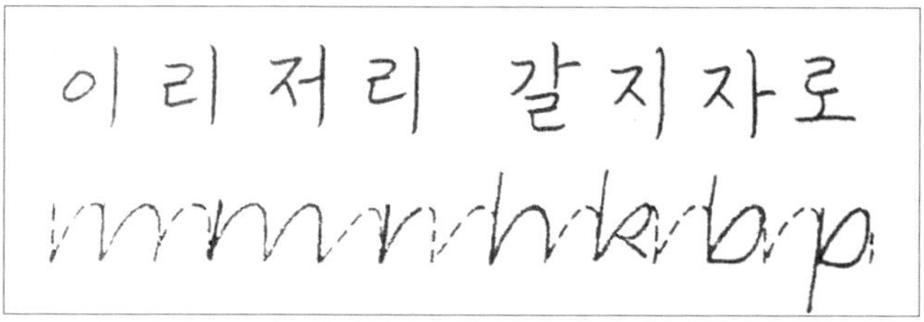

〈그림 4〉 국어의 수평적 횡서와 펜글씨

수평적 횡서법에서도 고빈도 모음에 수직획을 배당하는 전통을 그대로 유지하고 있지만, 이런 불일치(즉 수평적 횡서와 수직획 배당)이 <그림 4>의 아랫단에 보이듯이 펜글씨의 경우에도 잘 조화가 된다. 붓이건 펜이건 검지손가락을 수직적으로 움직이는 동작이 쉽기 때문이다. 수평적 횡서에서는 팔(목)이 '수평으로' 움직여 가면 기본 방향이 설정되고, 동시에 엄지와 검지와 장지로 쥔 펜만은 '수직으로' 움직이는 다른 동작이 가능하며 실은 이것이 세 손가락들의 수평 동작보다 더 쉬운 법이다.

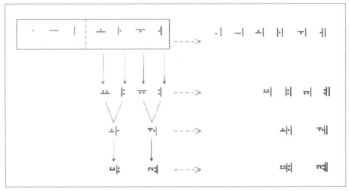

〈그림 5〉 모음자의 발달 전개도[1]

끝으로 모음에 대해 〈그림 5〉에 보인 중에 'ㅑ'와 'ㅕ'는 가능한 조합이며 중세국어에서도 필요한 글자였을 듯하지만, 세종이 제안하지는 않았다. 그러나 우리가 현대 방언음에서 '됐다'라든가 축약형으로 '바꼈다'를 표기할 필요성이 있을 때 이 글자들이 쓰인다는 점을 지적해 둔다.

----

1) 신상순·이돈주·이환묵(1988), p.87의 표를 단순화하고 방점으로 바꿔 인용.

4. 후기

안병희(개인적 면담)에 의하면 '훈민정음'이란 책에서 고전(古篆)과 비슷하다는 말을 한 것에 주목하며 자획의 모양에 대해 서예적으로 구별되는 모습이 있음을 세심히 관찰하도록 제안하였다. <그림 6A>에 보였듯이 훈민정음 판본에서 글자획의 시작과 끝이 아주 섬세하게 둥근 곡선이 되도록 판각되어 있다. 또 훈민정음으로 쓰여진 첫 번째 책인 이 책에서 '·[ʌ]'는 둥근 원으로 그려져 있다. 필자의 생각으로는 종/횡획의 시작과 끝도 둥글게 다듬어야 '·[ʌ]'의 둥근 원모양과 잘 조화가 된다는 서예 미관상 배려에서 <그림 6A>와 같은 각인을 했을 것으로 추정한다. 첫번 책이었고 훈민정음이 쓰인 양이 적었기 때문에 곡선의 둥근 모양들을 판각하는 수고가 가능했던 것이다. 그러나 위에서도 언급했고 <그림 6B>에서 보였던 것처럼, 아마 판각의 편의를 위해 획의 끝이 둥근 곡선이었던 것을 직각으로, '·[ʌ]'의 둥근 점은 직각의 끝을 가진 짧은 획으로 바꾸었다. 이렇게 툭툭 자르듯이 판각을 함으로서 많은 시간을 절약할 수 있었을 것이다. 조금 뒤에는 판각 편의만을 위하지 않고 그렇다고 아주 원초적 미관의 배려만 하지도 않고 절충을 하여, 이들 선은 다시 붓글씨를 위한 더 자연스러운 모습으로 <그림 6C>에 보이듯 보통 한자 서예의 해서체처럼 바뀌었다.

고 두 긼ㅅ훙 졍
티 텁 네ㅆ다 ᅙ

A. 훈민정음　　　B. 석보상절　　　C. 월인석보

〈그림 6〉

✤ 참고논저

강신항(1990), 훈민정음 연구(개정판), 성균관대학교 출판부.

김영기 Young-key Kim-Renaud, ed.(1997), The Korean Alphabet : Its History and Structure, University of Hawaii Press.

김완진(1975), 훈민정음 자음자와 가획의 원리, 어문연구 7 · 8, 이기문(1977 : 217~227) 재수록.

Ledyard, Gari (1966), The Korean Language Reform of 1446 : The Origin, Back-ground, and Early History of the Korean Alphabet, Ph.D. Dissertation, Berkeley : Univ. of California.

신상순 · 이동준 · 이환묵 (1988), 훈민정음의 이해, 한신문화사.

안병희(1997), "The Principles Underlying the Invention of the Korean Alphabet," in : 김영기 Young-key Kim-Renaud, ed.(1997 : 89~105).

유재원(1985), 우리말 역순사전, 정음사. 유창균(1966), "象形而字倣古篆"에 대하여, 진단학보 29 · 30. 이기문(1977 : 153~179)에 재수록.

이기문(1974), 훈민정음에 관련된 몇 문제, 국어학 2, 이기문(1977 : 200~216)에 재수록.

이기문(1997), "The inventor of the Korean alphabet," in : 김영기 Young-key Kim-Renaud, ed.(1997 : 11~30).

이기문 편(1977), 문자(국어학논문선 7), 민중서관.

이상억(1997), "Graphical ingenuity in the Korean writing system : With new reference to calligraphy," in : 김영기 Young-key Kim-Renaud, ed.(1997 : 107~116).

모방이 아니라 모략/질시
훈민정음은 몽골 팍바를 모방한 것이 아니라
문자적 독창성으로 창제된 것*

훈민정음이 한자를 '모방'해 창제되었다는 주장을 단지 6 가지의 비체계적인 '유사성'에 기초해서 할 수는 없다. 또 훈민정음이 팍바(Phagspa)자와 단지 5 글자가 모양과 발음에서 우연히 유사하다고 해서 '모방'했다고 결론지을 수도 없다.

훈민정음 창제의 공을 다른 곳으로 돌리려는 동기가 의아해진다. 음성기관의 자질적 기초와 음성적 자질을 체계적 가획으로 문자화한 것은 세종대왕의 독창적 천재성을 명백히 보이는 것이다.

일부 학자들이 훈민정음은 '창조'가 아니라 '모방'의 소산이라고 결론지으려는데 이를 설명할 이유를 아무리 찾으려 해도 이는 단지 '한글에 대한 시기/모략'이라고 볼 수밖에 없다.

---

* Inquiries into Korean Linguistics IV, 2011, 143-164에 영문 논문이 수록되었다. 여기 한국어 번역은 먼저 쓴 영문에 맞춰 번역한 문체라 좀 유려하지 못한 느낌이 들 것이다.

1. 팍바 문자가 훈민정음 초성/자음자의 모델이 될 수 있는가?

일부 학자들은 모방 가능한 원천에 대해 인근 국가의 문자들을 가정했다. Ledyard(1966)와 유창돈(1966)은 특히, 팍바 자음 ㄷ[d], ꥤ[l]를 한글 ㄷ[t]과 ㄹ[l]이 모방했을 모델로 지적했다. 그러나 그들은 한글 ㄹ[l] ㅅ[s] ㅈ[č] ㅌ[t']이 비슷한 모양의 팍바 문자 ㄹ[ŋ] ㅅ[o] ㅈ[o] ㅌ[j]]과 같은 음을 가지지 않는 점을 언급하지 않았다. 위의 우연한 유사성으로 보이는 예를 근거로 '체계적 일치'라는 주장을 정당화할 수 없다.(이상억 1997) 특히 팍바 자음 ㅁ[g]와 ㄹ[b]도 한글의 ㄱ[k]와 ㅂ[p]와는 체계상 아주 다르다.

훈민정음의 창제 때 팍바를 모델로 했다는 가설을 간략히 살펴보자. Ledyard(1966)는 한글의 핵심 자음들이 팍바 문자를 기반으로 했고, 다른 자음들은 아라마익 압자드(A-대문자로-aramaic abjad) 또는 원-시나이(Proto-Sinaitic) 문자에서 유래했다고 했다. 그는 한글의 자음체계의 일부가 몽고전자로 알려진 원나라시대의 팍바문자(1269?~1360)에서 유래한 5자에 기반을 두고 있다 한다.

Ledyard(1966)의 견해를 우선 보자. "단지 5개 문자만 팍바에서 채용되었다. 나머지 대부분의 자음은 이들로부터 자질파생(featural derivation)에 의해 훈민정음 해례에 설명된 바와 같이 창제되었다. 그러나 두 경우 어떤 자음이 기본인가가 다르다.

〈표 1〉 서방문자(그리스, 라틴)와 동방문자(브라믹, 한글)의 확산

Western ←		Phoenician	→ Brahmic			→ Korean
Latin	Greek		Gujarati	Devanagari	Tibetan*	
B	B	𐤁	બ	ब	བ	ㅂ, ㅁ
C, G	Γ	𐤂	ગ	ग	ག	ㄱ, (ㅇ)
Z	Z	𐤆	દ (ડ)	द (ड)	ད (ཌ)	ㄷ, ㄴ
L	Λ	𐤋	લ	ल	ལ	ㄹ
-	ϡ	𐤔	સ	स	ས	ㅈ, ㅅ

* HWP의 문자표 속 활자로 티벳문자(7세기)가 있고 또 유니코드 속에 팍바문자(13세기)가 있는데 90도로 돌려져 있다.
* 특히 치찰음(ㅅ, ㅈ)과 괄호 속 문자들에서 페니키안과 (아라마익을 거쳐) 브라믹까지의 정확한 일치를 주목하라. Z과 ㄷ, ㄴ의 차이를 볼 때, 티벳자에서 (팍바를 통해) 한글로 문자가 전해졌다는 주장은 그럴듯하지가 않다.

해례에서는 자형상 단순한 ㄱㄴㅁㅅㅇ이 기본이라고 말하며 나머지는 (ㆁㄹㅿ을 빼고는) 가획으로 더 만들었다고 한 반면, Ledyard는 음운론적으로 단순한 5자 즉 중국운학상 기본적인 ㄱㄷㄹㅂㅈ이 한글의 기본자라 했다. 다른 자음들은 이들 기본자에 획을 가감해 만든 것이라는 말이다. 그의 설명에선 팍바에서 취한 이 5 핵심 글자가 궁극적으로 ꡎབ, ꡂག, ꡊད, ꡙལ, ꡛས자[1]로부터의 파생이라는 것이다. 그래서 그의 설명에 의하면 그 글자들은 희랍자 Γ Δ Λ B와 라틴자 C/G D L B와 동족이다. 6째 기본자 ㅇ은 해례 설명과 같이 독창된 것이다."

1) 한국어 ㄹ에 대해 ꡙལ[l]을 Ledyard가 선택한 것은 어색한데, 팍바 ㄹ[ng] 자형이 분명히 더 비슷해 보이기 때문이다. 같은 식으로 한국어 ㅈ에 대해서도 ꡛས[s]을 숙고 끝에 대응시켰는데, 팍바 ㅈ[o] 자형이 더 비슷해 보이기 때문이다. 그는 의도적으로 문자보다는 발음을 대응시키려는 경향이 있었다.

ㅁ, ㄴ, ㅅ(m, n, s) 문자들의 소리를 낼 때 음성기관의 모양과 정확히 일치하는 형태의 문자로 인정하려면, 이 글자들이 세종에 의해 획을 체계적으로 증가했던 것이지; ㅂ, ㄷ, ㅈ와 같은 팡바문자에 기초해 '복사'한 것은 아니다. 복사 가설은 꽤 불거지는 불가능한 '우연의 일치'를 받아들이도록 강요하는 것과 같다.

〈표 2〉 en:Image:Phags-pa-Hangeul_cmparison.png의 팡바 문자와 한글 대조

*위 : '팡바 문자 ﹐[k], ᠊[t], ꡘ[p], ꡚ[s], ꡙ[l]와 그에 대응하는 것으로 여겨지는 한글 문자 ㄱ[k], ㄷ[t], ㅂ[p], ㅈ[ts], ㄹ[l].
*아래 : 중국어를 표현하기 위한 팡바 문자 ꡓ w, ꡤ v, ꡜ f 의 파생과 그의 변형 문자 ꡜ [h]
*왼쪽 : 밑에 기호를 덧붙인 ꡓ[w]와 유사한 중국어 표기용 한글 ㅱ w/m, ㅸ v, ㆄf 의 한글들은 기본자 ㅁ과 ㅇ에서 유래했다.
[위] 팡바 k, t, p, s, l과 한글 파생형 g, t, b, j, l [k, t, p, ts, l]. 두 [t]소리에 입술 (같은 왼쪽 위 튀어나온) 획에 주의. [밑] 팡바 문자의 변이형인 w, v, f의 파생형.

팡바의 기존 3자와 비슷한 모양에서 시작해, 이들에서 감획을 해서 거꾸로 문자들을 파생시키고, 그 문자에 의한 음의 생산이

음성기관의 모양에 정확히 귀결한다는 것[2]을 누가 미리 알고 진행할 수 있겠는가? 세종이 한글 창제의 천재라 믿는 필자도 세종이 그렇게 거꾸로 만드는 통찰력은 가졌다고 보기까지는 주저한다.

ㅁ, ㄴ, ㅅ(m, n, s) 같은 문자에 의해 표현되는 발음에서 음성기관의 모습인 글자로부터 시작하고 그 다음 단계로 ㅂ, ㄷ, ㅈ 같이 가획된 문자를 파생하는 것이 합당하며 상식에 맞다.

자연스럽고 합리적인 파생보다 '그럴싸한 우연의 일치'에 기반한 파생을 인정하도록 우리에게 요구하는 것은 궤변적이다. 그런 궤변의 원인을 설명하는 어떤 방법도 없어 필자는 아마 질시(envy)가 원인이 아닌가 한다.

그러나 훈민정음 해례의 의도적 오해 또는 오독이라고 하지 않고서는 위와 같은 결론에 도달할 수는 없다. 첫째 해례의 설명에서 한글이 음성기관 상형이란 점과 ㄱㄴㅁㅅㅇ 이 명백히 기본자라는 점이 밝혀져 있다. 예컨대, ㄴ(혀끝의 윗잇몸 뒤쪽에 닿는 모음)은 새 문자 시리즈 창조 과정에서 ㄷ에 앞서야 한다. 순서가 반대가 된다 해도 (이렇게는 되지 않았지만) 'n'의 생산과정에서 치조에 혀끝이 닿는 '그림'을 자형으로 만든 음성적 통찰력과 영감에 찬 독창성을 보인다.

---

2) 훈민정음의 발음기관 상형설과 정반대로 꾸며서 하는 말이다. 즉 팡바가 발음기관 상형으로 이끌었다는 식의 억설이다.

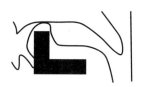

〈그림 1〉 ㄴ과 혀 모양의 일치

ㄴ에서 가획으로 ㄷ이 파생될 때 보이듯 세종은 아무렇게나 한 것이 아니고 반드시 체계적인 확장 방책을 썼다. 이 시점에서, 서예원칙이 동아시아에서 발휘한 중요한 역할에 대해 말해 보고 싶다. 서예와 붓이 동아 문화에서 가진 특별하고 중요한 위상을 고려할 때 우리가 분석에서 중대시해야 할 서예원리를 고려하는데 실패한다면 현대적 언어 분석에서도 과오와 오해를 저지를 수 있다고 믿는다. 이 실패는 특히 한글의 분석에서는 해로운 것이다. 바로 이 점이 Ledyard의 한글 기본자와 그 파생과정에 대한 설명에서 보인다.

위의 초점에서 흔히 간과되는 작은 부분이지만, 훈민정음에서 ㄷ은 위 왼쪽 구석너머로 작은 입술을 내민 모습이 있다. 이 입술은 위쪽 가획의 붓자국을 나타내는 것이다. 동아시아의 서예에 익숙한 사람들은 ㄷ의 모양을 쉽게 인식하고 이해할 것이다. 후론할 바와 같이, Ledyard(1998)는 그의 주장을 잘못 했는데 왜냐하면 ㄷ자의 형성에서 쓰인 꽛바자 ㅎ의 붓 닿는 첫 획의 붓끝 모양이라는 서예법을 고려하지 못했다.

다음은 더 따져 봐야 할, Ledyard에 의한 기본자와 파생자에 대한 설명이다.

치찰음 s ㅈ[ts]과 유음 l ㄹ[l]은 물론, (비유성, 비유기) 파열음 g ㄱ[k], d ㄷ[t], b ㅂ[p]는 중국운학에서는 기본음이지만 인도계 언어에서는 유성음도 기본음도 아니다.

비파열의 비음 ㅇ[ng], ㄴ, ㅁ과 마찰음 ㅅ은 무성파열음의 위 획들을 없앰으로서 파생된다. (ㄹ에서는 아무 글자도 바로 파생되지 않는다.) 이는 몇 가지 점을 밝혀 준다. 예컨대 ㅂ의 위 획들을 없앰으로서 ㅁ을 만들기는 쉽다. 그러나 ㅂ의 모양이 다른 파열음과 유사하지 않아서 거꾸로 어떻게 ㅁ에서 ㅂ을 파생시키는지는 분명치 않다. 만약 그들이 전통적 설명처럼 파생된 것이라면 우리들도 그 모두가 위에 비슷한 수직선 획이 있다고 예상해야 한다.

— 알파벳의 역사 : 위키피디아

첫째, ㅂ으로부터 ㅁ이 파생되었다는 위의 설명은 잘 해야 투기적 억측인 것이다. 더구나 서예에서의 균형 원칙을 적용시키면 ㅂ은 네모 위 두 구석에 획을 더해 만든 ㅁ에서의 자연적 확대다. 서예의 한 기본 원칙인 '균형'이 위 설명에 깔려졌다. 또 하나의 균형 잡힌 형태는 두 획이 더해진 ㅍ이다.

의심할 바 없이, 세종대왕은 한글 자음이 발음기관의 움직임을 그대로 반영하도록 혀가 치조나 연구개 부분을 접촉하는 모양이나 입모양을 본 따 제자를 시작했다.

이제 '모방'이냐 '창제'냐의 문제를 논하자. 보통 '모방'이 아니라 '창제'로 말하는 경우도 "한글이 (몽골이 아니라) **중국** 전자를 모방해서 만들었다"는 (정인지) 진술이 있어서, Ledyard나 유창균이 "한글이 **몽골** 전자의 모방으로 만들었다"고 오해하게 된 것이다. 아래에 보일 듯이 그런 해석은 결국 믿고 유지될 수 없는 것이다.

한글에 관해 언급할 때, 세종의 신하(정인지)가 문자 모습이 고전(古篆)과 비슷하다고 한 것을 기억하자. 사실 '새' 문자가 이미 '친숙한' 것을 닮았다고 말하는 것은 자연스럽다.

그러나 한글과 고전 사이의 유사성에 대한 정확한 진술은 다음과 같다. **자방고전**(字倣古篆) : 이는 "문자가 고전을 모방해 만들어졌다"는 뜻이다. 그러나 새 문자는 발음기관을 본 따 만들었다. 새로 만들어진 한글이 음성문자(어두, 어말자음과 모음에서)였던 만큼, 오래된 고전자처럼 다른 두 활자 세트 사이에서 형태의 우연한 유사성보다 차이점을 더 쉽게 알아챌 수 있다. 어쨌든 Ledyard(1997)은 단지 상상적 해석에 의해 '자방고전'이 "한글은 몽골 고전을 본 따 만들었다"고 잘못 이해한 것이다.

아래에 더 부연된 이유로서, '상형이자방고전'(象形而字倣古篆)의 뜻은 (훈민정음이) 발음기관을 본 따 만든 것이므로 그 결과 팡바 기원 가설보다 고대 중국 문자3)를 본 딴 것으로 봐야 할 듯하다.

1) 명왕조가 중국에 대두된 직후, 세종의 국가건설 전략과 정치적 배려는 훈민정음의 기원을 중국한자에 연결하여, 그로 하여 훈민정음을 원 왕조의 몰락해 가는 문자에 연결시켜서는 얻을 수 없는 정당성과 권위를 얻는 것이 합리적인 듯하다.

2) 훈민정음의 기원을 한자에 연관시키려 했고, 힘 있는 친명

---

3) 우연히 근래 Huwe(2010)는 꽤 동의할 만한 의견을 내놓았다. "자형성에서 문자는 고전을 모방했다"라고 하여, 모스크바 AKSE학회에서 필자와 똑같이 고전은 중국전자지 몽골문자는 아니었던 것이라는 해석을 했다.

진영을 만족시키려 했다면, 훈민정음이 고전 한자와 유사함을 강조하여 그의 목표는 아주 잘 성취되었다. 이는 방고전(倣古篆)이 이해된 정치적 맥락일 것이다.

3) 사각의 제약 내에서 음절을 만드는 것은 친숙한 한자에서 분명히 볼 수 있는 자질이며, 실제로 덜 알려졌고 덜 친숙한 팍바문자에서 이런 모델을 찾을 필요가 없다. 또 이렇게 다음과 같은 면을 보자. (인도의 수평적 전통과 대조적으로) 팍바는 수직적으로 쓰이며 또 음절적이라는 사실을 고려해야 한다면, 팍바문자는 한자를 본뜬 것이란 분명한 증거를 보여준다.

4) 더구나 훈민정음 음절의 모양 도안과 획순은 한자와의 조화를 많이 고려하였음을 보인다. 그런 관찰을 했을 때, 한글의 기원에 대한 설명에서 덜 친숙하고 더 떨어진 팍바 기원 가설을 보는 것보다 친숙하고 가까운 한자를 보는 것이 더 합리적이다.

위의 관찰은 이 논문 후반에서의 세계문자비교에서 한자와 한글을 비교할 때 기본획이 가장 많이 일치하는 사실을 보이는 데이터와 함께 더 전개될 것이다.

위 관찰은 한자 기원 가설을 암시하는 것보다는 팍바 기원 가설을 중지하게 하는 쪽이다. 더구나 훈민정음에 적용된 이 작업은 "비슷한, 그러므로 원형으로부터 복사된 것"이라는 주장이 완전 재평가를 당하는 듯하다.

한글이 한자와 유사성을 갖는 것은 자연스러울 뿐이다. 한글 창제 이전 한자는 우리가 1500년 이상 써 온 문자다. 한글이 꽤 친근하게 오랫동안 쓰여 온 표기체계에 의해 영향 받지 않았다면 아주 이상한 일일 것이다.

결과적으로 한글의 조형구조, 잘 구획된 네모 속의 형상화, 가로 세로 다 쓸 수 있는 능력 등은 한자와 같이 쓸 수 있는 조화를 달성한 탁월한 도안적 자질 속에 잘 반영되어 있다.

많은 한자본의 한국어역(언해본)은 한글 창제 초기에 발간되어, 한자와 한글이 조화롭게 같이 쓰일 수 있다는 분명한 전제를 보인다. 두 표기체계를 조화시키려는 것이 분명한 지혜는 여전히 흠모와 경이감을 자아낸다. 한글과 로마자를 같이 쓸 때 피할 수 없는 "이질감"과 아주 대조되는 사실이다.[4]

기본 획을 공유하고 있기 때문에 한글은 한자를 본떴다는 가설을 세운다면, 그런 것은 잘해야 흩어진 구름 위에 세운 가설이다. 첫째 어떤 형태 일치에서도 음의 일치까지를 발견할 수 없다. 수많은 형태 유사성이 다른 문자 체계에서도 비슷하게 발견된다. 이 상황은 단적으로 팡바가 한글의 모델이라는 근거 없는 논의와 꽤 같다. 팡바 가설은 잘 해야 독창적이 아니듯이, 한자 가설도 잘 해 봐야 비독창적이다.

한자 모델 가설이 궁극적으로 제기한 것(과연 어떤 X-모델 가설이

---

4) 물론 한국인들은 한자에 기초해서 그 행간에 써넣은 이두를 발달시켰다. 그러나 디자인의 범주로서 이두는 한자와 조화를 이루지 못한다. 한편 한글은 우수한 그래픽 디자인을 가진 포괄적 과학적 음성분석의 결과다.
한글은 다른 아시아 문자와 달리, 자음에서 모음을 성공적으로 떼어 냈다. 자음과 모음은 완전히 구별되고, 각 음절은 네모 속에 각 음의 산출시 발음기관을 그림처럼 보이는 음절 자음(무자음을 포함)을 체계적으로 시각화한다. 그리고 중앙 부분에 물리적 음성범주에 따라 자리 잡은 모음은 원순 중모음(ㅗ,ㅜ,ㅡ)은 자음 밑에, 다른 모음(ㅏ,ㅓ,ㅣ)은 자음의 바른쪽에 (모음)자리를 잡게 한다. 이런 점에서 한국 이두와 일본 가나는 둘다 한자에서 나왔지만, 분석적이고 시각적인 한글과는 그 성격상 근본적으로 다르다.

건)은 한글이 새로 보인 유일성과 독창성에 대한 또 하나의 도전
은 절대 아니다. 오히려 필자는 이 작업이 훈민정음의 경우 그런
X-모델 가설들의 비독창성과 논리적 약점임을 지적하는 데 일
조할 것을 바란다.

> Ledyard는 훈민정음 책에 몽고문자에 대해 일부러 신비한 얼굴을
> 한 점을 해석함으로서 대체로 다음과 같이 주장하며, 이 주장은 계획
> 된 듯하다. 세종은 팍바와 기타 음절문자들을 알았을 것이고, 그 문
> 자들은 다 분절적이었고, 한글에 대해 어떤 선행 형태도 제공하지 않
> 았다.
>
> —위키토피아 : 팍바

　Ledyard교수는 그의 논문에서 한글의 팍바 기원을 길게 썼기
에, 같은 책에서 한글은 음성기관의 모양에 기초했다는 분명한
동의를 했지만, 그 이후 그는 팍바 기원 가설의 대표적 지지자로
보여졌다.

　음성기관 모방설에 대한 분명한 동의와 나란히 팍바 기원설의
긴 논의를 보인 묘한 모순에 당면해, 지금 필자는 어떤 설명도
못한 채, Ledyard의 저작 속에 왜 모순된 견해가 보이는가에 대
한 심리적 설명으로 '시기'가 피치 못할 결론이라고 짐작한다.

　비록 누구든 모호한 자세를 취할 수는 있지만, 그는 두 기원을
동시에 옹호하는 것 같지는 않다. 이제까지 아무도 팍바 기원설
을 객관적으로 수긍할 증거를 제시하지 못했다.

2. 세계 문자들 가운데의 훈민정음 자형 :
어떤 문자에서도 흔히 쓰일 전형적 획의 세트 속에서

어떤 표기 체계의 문맥 속에서 수직, 수평, 사선들로 획의 종류 숫자들이 오히려 제한됐으며, 삼각형, 원, 그리고 여러 방향의 곡선들이 문자 속에서 흔히 쓰인다.5) (Lee, S.- O. 1997 : 109, 또한 Dürscheid 2006 : 87-88)6) 한 표기체계의 몇 요소가 다른 표기체계의 몇 요소와 '비슷한' 것을 발견했다고 놀랄 일은 아니다. 위에 언급한 기본획조차 흔히 쓰일 전형적 획의 세트로서, 단지 '모방'이 아니라 '유사성'의 준비된 후보가 될 것으로 이해된다.

필자는 한글과 다른 주요 표기체계(미노아, 페니키아, 그리스, 히브리, 브라미, 로만, 키릴, 중국 및 일본)간의 유사성을 봄으로서 '유사성'의 문제를 세계 표기체계의 넓은 문맥에서 탐구하려 한다.

아래는 한글과 다른 표기체계 간에 발견되는 시각적 유사성이다. 여기서는 일치 수를 높이기 위해 시각적 유사성에 우선권을 주고 음성대응은 무시된다. [ㅇ 14, ㄴ 13, ㅅ 13, ㄱ 11과 △ 11 들은 한글과 비슷한 모양들 중 시각적 유사성이 높다.]

---

5) 아주 비슷한 생각을 정초(鄭樵 1104-1162)의 통지(通志) 34권 육서략(六書略)에서 발견할 수 있다. 그중 기일성문도(起一成文圖 : 1획부터 문자가 생성된다는 도표)에 기본적 기하학적 요소 ㅡ ㅣ ╱ ╲ ┌ ㄱ ㄴ ㅣ ∧ ∨( )⌒ ⊓ ⊔ ⊏ ⊐ □ ㅇ · [그러나 △은 없음]들을 衡, 從, 邪, 反, 折, 轉, 側, 方, 圓, 偶라는 이름의 획과 연결했다.
6) Dürscheid(2006)는 "또한 수직, 수평, 사선, 원 등의 제한된 획들을 조합한 결과로 유사성들이 생겼다"는 필자(1997)의 견해를 인용하면서 한글창제에 대한 반대 가설이 증명되지 못했다는 의견에 동의했다.

<表 3 title>〈표 3〉 여러 문자의 획들 중 유사성 비교

Hangeul 1443/ total	ㅇ 14	ㄱ 11	ㅋ 2	ㄴ 13	ㄷ 7	ㅌ 8	ㄹ 1	ㅁ 6	ㅂ 0	ㅅ 13	ㅿ 11	ㅈ 2
Hiero-glyphic 30cBC 1								ㅁ [p]				
Minoan 30cBC 3	O [a]			ㄴ [li]							△ [ya]	
Phoenician 15cBC 3	ㅇ [o]			⊬ [l]		Ǝ [e]					△ [d]	
Ethiopian 8cBC 2		٨ [g]			[r]					٨ [l]		
Greek -7cBC- 6	O [ˤ]	ㄱ [p] EarlyG		⊬ [l] EarlyG		E [e] ModG				Λ[c, g, l] Early, ModG	△ [d]	
	ㅇ	ㄱ	ㅋ	ㄴ	ㄷ	ㅌ	ㄹ	ㅁ	ㅂ	ㅅ	ㅿ	ㅈ
Hebrew 6cBC 3	ㅇㅁ [s]	ㄱㄱ [d]						ㅁㅂ [m]				
cf.Arabic numerals	ㅇ 5	ㄱ 6								ㅅ 8		
Brahmi 3cBC 6	O [th]	(ㄱ7) [v]	(ㅋ [th])	L [u]	ㄷ [n]			ㅁ [b]		∧ [g]	△ [e]	
Berber 2cBC 4	O [r]				ㄷ [d]	(ㅌ8 [t])		ㅁ [r]		∧ [g]		
Iberian 2cBC 3								ㅁ [p]		∧ [l]	△ [t]	
Sassanide 3cAD- 2		ㄱ [r]			ㄷ [t]							
Carian ca.5cAD 4	ㅇ [o]					E [u]		ㅁ [e]			△ [l]	
Roman -6cAD- 2	O [o]				C	E [e]						
Cyrillic 9cAD 4	O [o]				C	E [e]				Λ, Л [l]	Δ, Д [d]	

	ㅇ	ㄱ	ㅋ	ㄴ	ㄷ	ㅌ	ㄹ	ㅁ	ㅂ	ㅅ	ㅿ	ㅈ
Yezidi 14cAD *5*	O [h]	ㄱ [t]		ㄴ [m]				ㅁ [d]			△ [g]	
Chinese 14cBC *7*		ㄱ/ㄱ Pinyin b	ㄱ tiao	ㄴyin (=隱)	ㄷfang Pinyin f	巳 chi	己	口 kou		ㅅren jen		大
Japanese 8cAD *5*		ㄱ [fu]	ㅋ [o]	ㄴ [re]	ㄷ [hi]	ㅌ [mo]		ㅁ [ro]		へ [he]		ㅈ [su]
Korean Idu, 6cAD *4*		ㄱ [ya]		ㄴ [sa]	ㄷ [ni]		ㄹ [i]	ㅁ [ko, ku]		ㅅ[tʌ], ∧[k], [yə]		ㅈ [myə]
Willis 1602 *4*	O TH	ㄱ D		L F	⊑ T					∧ A		
Cherokee 1821 *3*				**L** [tle]		**E** [kə]				**Λ** [ne]		

	ㅇ	ㄱ	ㅋ	ㄴ	ㄷ	ㅌ	ㄹ	ㅁ	ㅂ	ㅅ	ㅿ	ㅈ
Cree 1840 *5*		ㄱ [me]		L [ma]		Ɛ [kə]				Λ [pi]	△ [i]	
Fraser 1915 *5*	O [o]	ㄱ [ɯ]		ㄴ [l]		E [e]				Λ [ng]		
Pollard 1936 *6*	O [o]	ㄱ [h]		ㄴ [l]	ㄷ [tɕ]					Λ [z, y]	△ [tl]	
' *Phagspa*, 1243 *1*	ㅇ	ㄱ ꡢ [g]	ㅋ	ㄴ	ꡯ[d], cf.ꡯ[n]	ㅌ cf.ꡰ [dʑ]	ꡘ [l] cf.ㄹ [ng]	ㅁ ꡏ[b]	ㅂ ꡌ b	ㅅ cf.∧ [o] not initial	△	ㅈ ꡒ [s] cf.ㅈ [o]

---

7) ㄱ과 ㅋ은 브라미보다 약간 더 오래되고 지역적인 Kharosthi 문자에서 발견된다. 이 문자는 Mauryan 황제 아쇼카의 비문이 바위와 기둥에 쓰여진 고인도 기록에 쓰였다. Rogers(2005) p.205, Daniels and Bright(1996) pp.373~383.

8) 같은 베르베르 문자에서 투아레그의 현대판인 Tifinigh가 고대 베르베르에 없던 ㅌ [t]를 가지고 있다. Daniels and Bright(1996) p.114.

<표 3>에서 밑줄 근 것들이 다른 후보들보다 한글에 가깝다.
그들의 일치수 집계는 다음과 같다.

　　　　1 : 히에로글리픽, 팢바

　　　　2 : 로만, 이티오피안, Sassanides(Pehlevi)[9]

　　　　3 : 미노안(또는 크레타, 시프러스), 페니키안, 히브리, 이
　　　　　　베리안(프로토-히스파닉), *Cherokee*[10]

　　　　4 : 한국 이두, 키릴릭, Carian(Anatolian),[11] 베르베르
　　　　　　(리비안 포함), *Willis*[12]

　　　　5 : 일본 가나, Yezidi(Balti),[13] *Cree*,[14] *Fraser*[15]

　　　　6 : 중국 한자(Pinyin 포함[16]), 그리스, 브라미, *Pollard*[17]

---

9) 이란의 북부 Sassanides 왕조에서 Pehlevi 알파벳을 썼다. Février(1995) pp.295, 316.

10) 윌리스의 속기법과 Cherokee, Cree, Frazer, Pollard 같은 문자들의 이름은 이탤릭으로 썼고, 이들은 1443년 한글 창제 이후에 나타났다.

11) 첫 천년간에 쓰여졌고 서남 소아시아와 이집트에서 발견된 Carian 비문이 있었다.

12) John Willis는 1602년에 처음으로 음성학적 근거가 있는 속기체제를 만들었다.

13) Yezidi 암호문자는 카쉬미르 Baltistan에서 사용되는 문자다. Diringer(1996) p.209.

14) 또 Inuktitut 음절문자는 Cree의 모양과 합치함을 보인다. 선교사들이 이누이트 에스키모들에게 1856년 음절문자를 도입했다. 비슷하게 Chipewyan 음절문자도 1870년에 도입했다. Daniels and Bright(1996) pp.599~611.

15) 중국 주재 선교사 J. O. Fraser는 1915년 티베토버마어인 Lisu어에 대해 로마자 대문자를 이용해 인도식 문자를 만들었다.

16) Pinyin(拼音) 즉 Hanyu Pinyin(漢語 拼音)은 1958년 이후 북경관화의 로마자 표기체제로 현재 널리 쓰인다.

17) 중국 주재 선교사 S. Pollard는 서부 Hmong의 Miao족을 위해 기하학적 문자를 만들었고 1936년에 개선안도 내놓았다.

<표 3> 속에 적용 됐듯이 '합치'의 더 좁은 범주를 적용한다면, 팡바에서 발견되는 제일 가까운 형이 ㄷ 하나뿐이었다. 한글 ㄹ에 대해 팡바 ㄹ[ng]이 回ㅁ[l]을 합치시키는 것보다 더 유사하다. ㄹ[ng]을 回ㅁ[l]에 대응시킨 레댜드의 선택이 음의 일치제약에 의한 것이라 해도, 팡바 ㄹ[ng]이 한글 ㄹ에 그 모양이 더 합치하는 우수성은 레댜드 교수의 주장을 약하게 만든다. <표 1>의 페니키안에서 유래한 브라미가 6개 합치를 공유하는 반면 (티벳과) 팡바는 오직 1개의 합치만 보인다.

위의 통계에서 4부터 6의, 한국 이두, 일본 가나, 한자는 의미가 있다고 보인다. 위 데이터가 보이듯이 이 셋은 한글 창제에 영향을 주었던 후보가 될 수 있다. 흥미로운 사실로 한자가 이두보다 더 한글과 합치됨이 여실히 보인다. 그리스와 키릴 문자가 서로 눈에 띄게 유사성을 보이는데, 키릴 형제가 새 문자를 창제할 때 그리스 문자를 모델로 했기 때문에 놀랄 일도 아니다.

한글이 이두나 가나 같은 가까운 곳의 모든 문자들보다 그리스 문자와 더 합치하는 형태가 많다는 점을 지적해야 한다. 우리가 "많은 유사형, 그러므로 모방 복사"라는 식의 주장을 따른다면 그 (모방)영향이나 (복사)모델의 후보들 중에 오히려 그리스의 문화 판도는 가장 먼 곳임에도 불구하고 한글이 그리스문자를 본땄거나 복사했다는 지탱하지 못할 결론에 도달하게 한다.

ㄴㄷㄹㅁㅅ과 한자 ㄴ ㄷ ㄹ ㅁ ㅅ은 거의 완전히 같다고 주목할 수 있다. 중국어 주음부호 ㄷ[f]은 한국어 ㄷ[t]와 거의 모양이 같다. 이런 합치는 한자가 세상의 어떤 문자체계보다 수가

많다는 점을 생각할 때 놀랄 것이 없다.

우리가 일본어로 돌아가도 비슷한 합치를 발견한다. 한국 이두 尼[ni]와 일본 가나 比[hi]에서 각각 비롯되었을 ㄴ 모양을 가지고 있다. 한편 ㅁ은 같은 몸에서 유래됐고 국어 려[ryo]와 일어 [ro]를 각각 나타낸다. 야 也[ya]에서 한국 ㅋ, 由[yu]에서 일본 ユ도 생겼다.

그러나 한글과 다른 표기체계 사이에서 찾거나 보여지는 모든 현저한 유사성에 대해 사실 그런 관찰된 유사성으로부터 어떤 의미 있는 결론을 낼 수 없다.

인류역사에서 발견되는 표기체계상의 모든 증명된 '모방'에 대해, 말하자면 제2의 창제가 세상에 유일하고 선행된 예가 없는 음성자질 표기체계라는 단순한 이유로 세종이 한글을 창제하는 데 선행모델이 된 것을 찾으려는 시도는 무의미한 바, 세상에 이와 같은 것은 없기 때문이다.

이 유일성에 대한 단순한 사실을 마음에 두고 한글 창제의 선행 모델이 된 것을 찾으려는 레댜드 교수에 의한 한글의 팡바 모델설은 애초에 무의미한 노력 같은 모든 과거의 학자적 시도는 처음부터 불운한 시도라는 것을 알게 한다. 이는 그가 한글은 음성기관의 형상에 근거했다는 견해에 명백히 동의했음에도 돌이킬 수 없는 것이다.

그래서 왜 아직 그런 시도가 있는가? 왜 공의 인정이 유일성과 독창성에 기인하는 경우 학자들이 그 공을 인정할 수 없는가? 한글이 '시기'의 정당한 대상이라 하더라도, 시기는 학문의 바탕이 될 수는 없다.

세종의 천재성의 산물로서 한글이 세상에서 유일하고 전례가 없는 음성자질표기체계를 보여 주었다. Bell의 Visible Speech보다 오래전에 세계 최초의 Visible Speech를 만든 것이다.

그것은 칭송 받을 만한 '문자적 독창성과 천재성'을 구현하였고, 그래서 감히 '시기'라고 규정한다.

❖ 〈참고문헌〉과 〈부록〉은 pp.127~132의 영어 쪽에 보임.

십장생 문자도(十長生 文字圖)

십장생(十長生)은 열 가지 장생불사의 표상에 해당하는 물상들이다. 보통 거북[龜]·사슴[鹿]·학[鶴]·소나무[松]·불로초(不老草)·산[山]·[水]내[川]·돌[石]·해[日]·구름[雲]들을 꼽고, 또는 달[月]·대나무[竹]·복숭아[桃]로 바꿔 넣기도 한다.

다음 그림은 글자로 그린 문자도인데, 자의로 만든 형상은 없이 사천사서출판사(四川辭書出版社, 1991)의 갑금전예대자전(甲金篆隸大字典)에 나오는 상형문자로만 배치한 작품이다. 다만 불로초만은 한 글자로 된 문자가 없기 때문에 그 줄기 모양에 초록색으로 불로(不老)라고 써 넣었다.

문자론을 연구하는 학생들에게 상징(symbol)의 의미와 기능을 탐구해 보도록 거들려는 의도의 작업이었다. 돌석자의 ㅁ이나 ㅂ[石자의 전자이형(篆字異形)에 ㅂ 모양이 나타남]속에 한글의 ㄱ~ㅂ을 넣어 그 자형들의 가획(加劃)확산적 내재질서도 보이려 했다.

그리고 '낙관(落款)' 자리에, 작가와 감상자가 소통할 수 있는 이메일 주소를 서명처럼 써서 새 시대적 기법을 회화에 처음 도입하는 시도도 해 보았다.(sangoak@snu.ac.kr)

동물원 문자도(動物園 文字圖)

갑금전예대사전(甲金篆隸大辭典, 四川辭書出版社, 1991)을 살펴 보면 중국 갑골 금석 전예서체 속에, 특히 동물에 관한 흥미로운 상형화 작업이 누천년 녹아 있다. 동물형상들의 추상화 과정에 있어 문자론이나 화화적으로 세계의 어떤 다른 지역 상형문자보다 한자가 꽤 합리적이라고 설득한다.

이 동물원 문자도는 그 중 240여 자를 뽑아 선보인 것인데 흥미있는 자형을 많이 넣다 보니 동물원 속이 무척 복잡해졌다. 그래서 십장생에 쓰인 거북[龜]·사슴[鹿]·학[鶴]은 뺐다. 牛馬羊猪(豚)는 물론 犬(狗) 猫 狐 狼[이리 랑] 猿 熊 獲 과 虎 獅子 豹 狸[삵 리] 駱駝 및 象 麒麟 犀[코뿔소 서] 河馬 등, 또 십이지(十二支)의 子(鼠) 丑 寅 卯(兔) 辰(龍) 巳(蛇) 午 未 申 酉(鷄) 戌 亥, 어류의 魚 鯉 沙魚 鯨 그리고 鰐魚, 조류의 鳥 烏 鴨 鳩 雀 孔雀 雁 鷹 鵝 雛 그리고 상상의 새 朋과 鳳[龍과 함께 실존치 않는 동물이지만 이 동물원에 특례 편입]. 기린 밑에 흑백 띠 무늬의 얼룩

말도 숨어 있다.

갈之자의 마디마다 ㅅ과 ㅈ을 포함한 ㅊ이나 ㅋ, ㅌ, ㅍ 자의 모양이 나타난다. 또 ㅇ, ㅎ까지 한글의 ㅅ-ㅎ을 다 넣어 자음자 형들의 내재 질서를 더 보이려 하였다. 之자는 발음이나 모습이 z와 흡사하여 zoo의 첫 자리를 차지했다. ZOO자형으로 화면에 생겨난 각 구획들은 하늘만 빼고 동물원의 각 부류별 울타리며 우리며 칸막이라 할 수 있다. 그리고 '낙관' 자리에 이메일 주소 를, 토끼 옆에는 홍콩의 신년 장식을 떼어다 부착해 보았다.

(sangoak2@gmail.com)

여기 처음 두 그림은 한자, 특히 동물 관계 문자의 상형성에 주목하고 글자 그대로 조합하여 회화성을 살린 작품들이다. 그 틈틈이 한글의 조형성도 주목하여 처음 ㄱ~ㅂ, 그 다음에는 ㅅ~ㅎ 자음을 그림 속에 배치하였다.

다음 세 번째 그림도 같은 흐름인 문자에 관한 내용으로, 우선 한글의 모음 구성을 방사선형 확장식으로 보여서, 위 자음들에 이어 한글을 다 완성하였다. 숫자 줄 밑에 시도한 한글의 자음과 모음에 대한 디지털식 표기 줄도 로마자 경우보다 그 가능성이 훨씬 유리한 문자임을 증명하였다.

배경으로 자생적 원시 문자 발생지역만을 표시한 지도에도, 한글은 독창적 발생의 경우이므로 당당히 등재된 것이다.

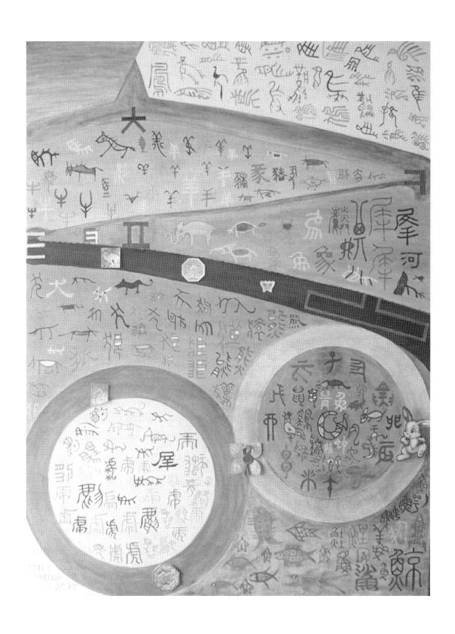

동물원 문자도(動物園 文字圖)　　59

상형문자 발생지도 및 기호체계도

언어학의 문자론에서 전세계 상형문자의 발생을 보면, 메소포타미아 및 동지중해 지역, 이집트, 인도, 중국, 마야(멕시코 등) 문명 지역이 꼽힌다. 나머지 후기 문자들은 이들에서 유래했더라도 상형성이 약해져서 회화적인 요소가 사라진 형상이다. 그 중 중국 한자는 전서나 금석문에서는 특히 상형성이 널리 살아 있다. 그대로 옮겨도 회화의 요소가 될 정도다.

한글의 자음자 중 ㄱ, Δ, ㅇ은 그 형상을 지구상 다른 지역에서 같게 쓴 대로 그려 넣었다. 한글의 모음자는 천지인(天地人)을 상형하여 그 기본요소를 복합 사용하여 21자까지 확산시켰다. 그 공통 기반을 가운데 푸른 네모 속에 집약하여 놓았다. · (점)은 종횡으로 다 연결되어 문자를 만들 수 있다.

ㅂ자의 모양 속에 숫자와 한글 자음, 영자를 써넣었다. 숫자는 지구의 경도에 맞춰 시간대를 표시하였다. 한글 경우 14자를 다 표현할 수는 있으나 자형의 변개가 필요했다. 그러나 영자의 K,

M, N, O(D와 같아짐), Q, R, T, V, W, X, Y, Z는 나타내기가 어렵다. 영자의 14개가 되고 12개가 안 되는 쪽이므로 거의 반이 불가능한 형국이다.

바코드와 QR 코드도 넓은 의미의 현대 문자요 기호체계다. 초코렛 포장지에 나와 있는 12지 관계 동물과 그 상형자도 중국에 붙여 놓았다. 그 외에 동전 모양과 술병 라벨 모양 초코렛 포장지도 문자가 담겨 있어 해당 지역에 붙여 놓았다. 인도양 아래쪽 빈 공간은 김성실의 작품을 빌어 메워 보았다. 다 주변에 떠도는 자료들을 이용해서 공간 확충 작업을 한 것이다.

남미는 상형문자가 존재치 않아, 북미의 마야 문명에 나타난 문자가 유일한 경우였다.

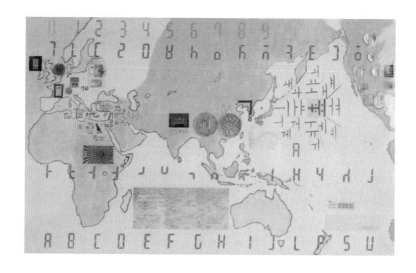

CONTENTS

The Hidden Code in Designing Hangeul :
Royal Grace Unrealized for Over 570 Years

In the situation of SF I first met 이도(李祹, Lee Do), a designer in his forties, absorbed into his work throughout the night, relying on a light of a candle. He was making various strokes with finely ground chinese ink on the traditional Korean paper. Horizontal, vertical, diagonal and dotted lines, in addition to circles and dots were visible; he was devising a new writing system.

He was seized with the thought to at least let people know ㄱ with a sickle in hand.

Assuming most farmers are right-handed, if a sickle was held with the right hand, a shape of ㄱ would be present before them. On the other hand, if a sickle was held with the left, the shape of a Γ, which is used by the Greeks and Russians[1] would

1) Not only Russia, but also many Slavic areas are receiving disadvantage by

be shown. Try to do so with a sickle! This simple approach seemed as if it was devised under deep consideration and pity for the uneducated general public.

However, he was more than a designer of simple ideas. Turning into my seventies, I was able to look into the underlying meaning this genius man in his forties, had put into work. I also had a feeling that he would create a design of tremendous value in a matter of years. It would be a great mistake to judge him merely as a man who determines right and left with a sickle; he had deeper intentions and plans.

ㄱ vs Γ

Having drawn Γ several times with a brush, he seemed to have set his decision on the shape ㄱ, because Γ takes two strokes, while ㄱ takes only one. Drawing a ㄱ would save people several tenths of a second than those drawing a Γ. This is a good example of how good designs bring great benefits, in contrast to bad designs that accompany harm. Likewise ㄴ was chosen because ㆞ needs one more stroke.

---

the spread of Cyril letters, which were created under a bad decision of the Cyril brothers to take gamma from the Greek alphabet. From the four ㄱ ㄱ ㄴ ㆞, Lee Do decided to use ㄱ and ㄴ, while the Roman alphabet used L, and the Chinese characters, ㄴ and ㄱ.

ㅋ vs F

Subsequently, he chose the shape ㅋ after a few brush strokes. He intuitively added a second stroke to ㄱ to create ㅋ. Without knowing that in the far foreign lands of the West, a shape of F with three strokes was widely used, this genius has saved us much time by creating the opposite, ㅋ, with two strokes. It is definitely something to be thankful of and deserves great admiration!

ㅁ 〉 ㅂ 〉 Xㅂ 〉 ㅂ↰ㅍ

cf. ㄹ/ㅌ

A few days later, I met him again and saw the completed chart of letters. I especially asked why he chose ㅍ instead of ㅁ 〉 ㅂ 〉 ㅂ, which was the expected pattern. He laughed and said that people would have thought ㅁ evolved from the Chinese character 口 meaning 'mouth', and if he chose ㅂ, people will regard it to have evolved from 日, the Chinese letter meaning 'day.' Yet, another profound consideration was hidden behind his notion of being different from China; had ㅂ been chosen, it would have been hard to differentiate from ㄹ and ㅌ, when written very small.

Confused by the unexpected reference to 'small' writings, I asked him what he meant. He already had in mind to create combinations of letters, or characters, to fit into a square, for the ease of reading. Indeed, 를 is much easier to read than a line of ㄹㅡㄹ. Nonetheless, the combinations would end up looking very small and seem complicated.

He was already writing down characters such as 를, 틀 and comparing them, worried by the fact that they looked too similar. Rather than adding a third similar character such as 루:투: 푸, he decided that 플 or 푸 would make the system less complicated. Deep thoughts and effort were definitely put into the making of ㅍ!

Moreover, ㆁ was introduced to avoid the confusion possibly caused by a candidate (ㄱ〉 ㅋ〉) ㅋ among similar ㄹ and ㅌ. ㅋ was not chosen although it is quite natural addition of a stroke to ㄱ but looks too similar to ㄹ and ㅌ. His selection of different looking ㆁ is clever because its sound /ng/ occurs only in the syllable final position. /ng/ never occurs in the syllable initial position and it is in the complementary distribution with dummy symbol ㅇ which was already included in Hunminjeoneum.

Lee Do would not have known this himself, but his decision of ㅍ over ㅂ made it possible to write the letters ㄱ to ㅂ in a single rectangular box.

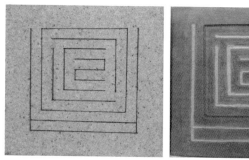

Next has included ㅋ, ㅌ, ㅍ, putting letters ㄱ to into a larger rectangular box. With ㅂ, it would have been hard to do so, but ㅍ has made it possible. This hidden identity that Lee Do himself would not have known, was conceived from the perfect combinations of vertical and horizontal lines. The formativeness of Lee Do's letter system was proven carefully through the standard of squares.

The rest, ㅅ, ㅇ, ㅈ, ㅊ, and ㅎ, can also be integrated into a single form.

This form symbolizes the keyhole that would open the path to the next level. It is fascinating to reveal the hidden "codes" behind this form.

Leaving the story of the keyhole for later and going back to Lee Do's careful design process, Lee Do would have known the four directions,[2] ㄷㄱㄲㄴ, when deciding to use ㄷ. From the four, by adding a stroke to ㄴ and creating ㄷ, he abandoned the other three ㄱㄲㄴ. Again, he was trying to minimize similarity between the letters for easier differentiation. Furthermore, by leaving the right side open, it would allow

2) Much later in 1927, Park Yong Man compiled <됴션말 독본 첫 책> and <됴션말 교과셔 둘재 책>, and introduced ㄱ for a writing symbol of the English alphabet "d" and the Japanese character "ㄱ", in addition to ㄴ for the English alphabet v and the Russian letter н. Thus, he established auxiliary letters to be used to write loanwords. cf) Hong Yoon Pyo (2013) 한글이야기, 1 한글의 역사, p.296. Furthermore, there are ㄷ, ㄴ for Chinese characters; Roman letters have U, but this has evolved from V, rather than ㄴ.

vowels such as ㅓ, ㅕ to be placed inside the opening.

cf. Lee, Sang-Oak (1997) Graphical Ingenuity in the Korean Writing System : With New Reference to Calligraphy. In Young-Key Kim-Renaud ed., The Korean Alphabet : Its History and Structure. , Honolulu : University of Hawaii Press. 107-116. Also in 이상억 (2002) "훈민정음의 자소적(字素的) 독창성," 고영근 외 '문법과 텍스트,' 서울대 출판부. [= Korean translation of Lee, Sang-Oak 1997].

Lee Do named the shapes until now as "consonants", and named its complementary dots, horizontal and vertical lines to be "vowels." These ·, ㅡ, ㅣ shapes are also used in the Chinese characters. When creating letters, there is a limitation to strokes such as horizontal, vertical, diagonal lines, circles, etc, and therefore, a systematic similarity is somewhat inevitable.

Originally, ㅣ+·, ·+ㅣ, ·+ ㅡ, ㅡ +· combinations developed into ㅏㅓㅗㅜ, and again expanded to ㅑㅕㅓㅕ, ㅗ ㅛㅜㅠ, ㅐㅔㅒㅖ, ㅘㅝㅙㅞ, ㅢㅚㅟ. Steps of this process are layed out as follows:

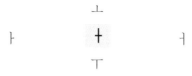

Lets add a layer of secondary vowels.

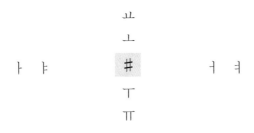

ㅛ
ㅗ
ㅒ
ㅏ ㅑ   ㅓ ㅕ
ㅜ
ㅠ

Next, green and blue letters are added.

ㅛ
ㅘ   ㅗ   ㅖ
ㅏ ㅑ   ㅓ ㅕ
ㅒ   ㅜ   ㅝ
ㅠ

Then, red letters of ㅚ, ㅟ are included.

ㅚ
ㅛ
ㅘ   ㅗ   ㅖ
ㅏ ㅑ   ㅓ ㅕ
ㅒ   ㅜ   ㅝ
ㅠ
ㅟ

Lastly, four letters, ㅒ, ㅖ, ㅙ, ㅞ are added.

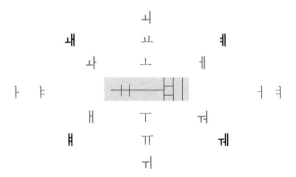

The key shape in the center can make all shapes of vowels.

Meanwhile, ㆍ, ㅡ, ㅣ, that are the basic shapes representing ㆍ (天 하늘), ㅡ(地 땅), ㅣ (人 사람) can be combined to create ㅓ. This completes the 21 vowels used in modern Korean, but there also used to be ㆍㅣ which is obsolete now.

1) ㅏ　ㅓ　　ㅗ　ㅜ
2) ㅏ ㅑ ㅓ ㅕ　ㅗ ㅛ ㅜ ㅠ
3) ㅏ ㅑ ㅓ ㅕ　ㅗ ㅛ ㅜ ㅠ　ㅐ　ㅔ　　ㅘ　ㅝ
4) ㅏ ㅑ ㅓ ㅕ　ㅗ ㅛ ㅜ ㅠ　ㅐ　ㅔ　　ㅘ　ㅝ
　　　　　　　　　　　　　　　　　　　　　ㅚ　ㅟ
5) ㅏ ㅑ ㅓ ㅕ　ㅗ ㅛ ㅜ ㅠ　ㅐ ㅒ ㅔ ㅖ　ㅘ ㅙ ㅝ ㅞ
　　　　　　　　　　　　　　　　　　　　ㅚ ㅢ ㅟ

Now, imagine putting the "key" found above into the consonant "keyhole" mentioned earlier. Of course, it is hard to say that Lee Do had intented this. However, think of it as finding the secret to this amusing combination of shapes. The interesting relationship between the Korean consonants and vowels, which were hidden in the Korean alphabet, can be peeked into with this hidden design code.

Returning to Lee Do's plan create combinations of letters for the ease of reading, each syllable is systematically visualized within the square with syllable consonants (including null) graphically describing the speech organs in the production of each sound and taking the central position and the vowels positioned according to physical phonetic criterion, below the consonant for vowels with vertical lines (ㅏ, ㅐ, ㅑ, ㅒ, ㅓ, ㅔ, ㅕ, ㅖ, ㅣ) and to the right of the consonant for other vowels with horizontal lines (ㅗ, ㅛ, ㅜ, ㅠ, ㅡ, also ㅘ, ㅙ, ㅚ, ㅝ, ㅞ, ㅟ, ㅢ). When there are final consonants in a syllable, they are written at the bottom.

∞:ㅣ

흙, 닭

빗, 활

These units of syllables composed into squares are also able to be found in Chinese writing system. Characters such as 江, 部, 忠, 碧, etc, are examples of how this structure was used prior to Lee Do.

The Korean Alphabet

An Optimal Featural System with Graphical Ingenuity

Abstract

This paper will argue that the structure of the Korean alphabet, called **Hangeul** (=Hangŭl), is logical and systematic. It is a notable fact that the vowels are based on three philosophical symbols for Heaven, Earth, and Human, and the consonants are based on the shapes of speech organs.

De Francis (1989) claims Alexander Melville Bell's "Visible Speech"(VS) is featural because it consistently takes a C-shaped symbol for *consonant*. As a result this *consistent* iconic alphabet ends up with shapes that prove confusing with so many similar C-shapes and cannot be used as a universal phonetic writing system. Although VS was a faithful featural script, Bell failed to understand where to leave this faithfulness. But King

Sejong, the creator of the Korean alphabet, knew how to make a featural system optimally practical. Sproat(2000) classified Hangeul as "an intelligently constructed segmental alphabet." However, I believe that Hangeul is not just a segmental alphabet, but the **optimal featural system; that is, more than** a segmental system that comes close to being a featural system but intentionally avoids becoming completely featural by allowing a variation like ㅍ [p^h].

1. Introduction

According to the annals of the Joseon dynasty, King **Sejong** the Great, invented the first version of the Korean alphabet, Hangeul, which was originally called the Hunmin jeong-eum (lit. The Correct Sounds for the Instruction of the People). He alone created the alphabet in 1443 and spent three years testing it. (Lee, Ki-Moon 1992) The alphabet was promulgated in 1446 in a book with the same name as the alphabet, Hunmin jeong-eum . This book was written in Chinese characters, which look very complicated. Which is why many foreigners may have had the impression that the book was Chinese. Like anything else written in Korea at the time, King

Sejong's book was written in Chinese because Korea didn't have their own indigenous written language. However, from the book, frequent examples of the new alphabet Hunmin jeong-eum, which is comparatively simple, is inserted in the text. Also, it is unique that the creation of the new alphabet was recorded in a book. These two facts are remarkable aspects that occurred for the first time in human history. [cf. The faximilied Hunmin jeong-eum at the end of this article] Later, Eonhae (Ŏnhae), a new edition of the same book featuring a translation of the text from Chinese to Middle Korean, was published. Many parts of the original book Hunmin jeong-eum were written in the new Korean script. This is an epoch of Korean history where there was a transition from the borrowed Chinese writing to the indigenous Hunmin jeong-eum.

The vowel letters are based on the three philosophical symbols for the trinity ∶ · (Heaven), ― (Earth), and ㅣ (Human). These are typically the limited set of strokes (vertical, horizontal, and short lines, which later became dots) frequently used in many other alphabets. All the vowels in the Korean language are combinations of dots, horizontal and vertical lines. These signs are balanced into the *Yang* (bright) sounds and *Yin* (dark) sounds for harmony, which according to Taoism are the universe's two opposing energies.

The Heaven	The Earth	The Human
(*Yang* bright, male)	(*Yin* dark, female)	(neutral)
Round dot	Level	Standing
· ` ₋	― ― ―	❘ ❘ ❘

King Sejong created a separate symbol for each vowel phoneme. There are eleven vowels shaped after symbols that represent the most important elements in eastern cosmology. This remarkable accomplishment is as important as the figurative representation of *consonant* features, which will be addressed later in this paper. Prior to the 15th century, no writing system with a full representation of the vowels was known in all of Asia. Indian alphabets, for example, which were familiar to Koreans through Buddhism, incorporate the vowel "a" into the *consonant* symbols and represent other vowels with diacritics. The creation of individual letters for vowels was a landmark, literary innovation unprecedented in East Asia. The analysis of a syllable by tripartite C-V-C (onset- nucleus-coda, where "C" and "V" represents "consonant" and "vowel", respectively) was creatively introduced by breaking the long tradition of bipartite C-rhyme(=VC) fundamental to Chinese phonology. It is quite a remarkable recognition of exact syllable structure needed for Middle Korean phonology, which was unlike Chinese phonology without proliferated final consonants.

It is a notable fact that the consonant letters are based on the shapes of various positions the speech organ makes when making the respective sound. Uniquely among the world's alphabets, the consonants are autonomously derived from this core ㄱㄴㅁㅅㅇ as a featural system. The phonetic background of the script Hunmin jeong-eum is clearly explained in the book Hunmin jeong-eum. According to *Hunmin jeong-eum Haerye* ("Explanations and Examples of the Correct Sounds for the Instruction of the People") the basic consonant symbols are schematic drawings of the speech organ's position articulating the sound. These aspects of imitating exact physiological figures are the 'Graphical Ingenuity' of this alphabet that cannot be encountered in any other writing system including Bell's *Visible Speech* in the West.

Origin of the shapes of basic consonants

| velar consonant ㄱ | alveolar consonant ㄴ | dental consonant ㅅ | bilabial consonant ㅁ | glottal consonant ㅇ |

Fig. 1. Origin of the shapes of basic Korean consonants : Symbolization of speech organs. Cited from Sisayongosa ed. (1983).

Consonants articulated at the same place in the mouth share the same basic graph. Then, if one of these consonants has the added feature of aspiration, the symbol for that consonant is written with an additional stroke. Compare, for example, the symbols of the Roman alphabet, in which nothing in the shapes of the letters indicate how the phonemes are articulated. For example, pairs of letters such as *t* and *d* provide no clue that the two sounds they represent are related in any way, namely that both are articulated in the alveolar region.

	Basic letters	Addition of a stroke (plosive)	(aspirated)	Doubling (glottalized)	Variation/ Added strokes
Velar	[ㆁ (ŋ)]	ㄱ (g)	ㅋ (k)	ㄲ (kk)	
Alveolar	ㄴ (n)	ㄷ (d)	ㅌ (t)	ㄸ (tt)	ㄹ (r, l)
Bilabial	ㅁ (m)	ㅂ (b)	ㅍ (p)	ㅃ (pp)	
Dental	ㅅ (s)	ㅈ (j)	ㅊ (č)	ㅉ (jj)	
Glottal	ㅇ [null]		ㅎ (h)		

ㅇ [null] appears only in the initial position when a syllable starts with a vowel. Since no other alphabet has ever imitated the shapes of actual speech organs (except 口 representing the mouth in Chinese character), this is a very novel idea with the articulatory phonetic explanation, which drastically preceded Bell's *Visible Speech*. Although some scholars have attempted to draw coincidental and nonsystematic connections between a few of the letters in Hunmin jeong-eum and those of neighboring writing systems, these apparent similarities are the result of the limited nature of the set of strokes (vertical, horizontal, and slated lines, and circles) frequently used in an alphabet.

2. 'Phags-pa Script as a Possible Model for the Korean Consonants

Ledyard (1966) and Yu Chang-gyun (1966) have suggested 'Phags-pa script as a possible model for the Korean alphabet, in particular, the 'Phags-pa consonants [d] for Korean [t]. However, other letter shapes, like Korean ㅅ[s], ㅈ[č], and ㅌ[t'], do not have the same sound value as the similar 'Phags-pa letters ㅅ[o], ㅈ[o], and ㅌ[j]. With only this much coincidental similarity, nobody can fairly claim that there is systematic correspondence. Let us briefly introduce the hypothesis of 'Phags-pa script as a possible model for the Korean alphabet.

Some scholars, including Gari Ledyard, believe that the core consonants of Hangeul were taken from the earlier 'Phags-pascript with the other consonants derived from Aramaic abjad or Proto-Sinaitic. (Cf. History of the alphabet from

Wikipedia) Ledyard suggests that portions of its consonantal system may be based on half a dozen letters derived from Tibetan via the imperial 'Phags-pa alphabet of the Yuan dynasty of China known as the *měnggǔ zhuānzì* (Mongol seal script).

"Only five letters were adopted from 'Phags-pa, with most of the rest of the consonants created by featural derivation from these, as described in the account in the Hunmin jeong-eum Haerye. However, which letters the basic consonants were differs between the two accounts. Whereas the Haerye implies that the graphically simplest letters ㄱㄴㅁㅅㅇ are basic, with others derived from them by the addition of strokes (though with ㆁㄹ △ set apart), Ledyard believes the five phonologically simplest letters ㄱㄷㄹㅂㅈ, which were basic in Chinese phonology, were also basic to hangeul, with strokes either added or subtracted to derive the other letters. It was these five core letters which were taken from the 'Phags-pa script, and ultimately derive from the Tibetan letters ཀ ད ལ བ ས. Thus they may be cognate with Greek ΓΔΛΒ and the letters C/GDLB of the Latin alphabet. A sixth basic letter, ㅇ, was an invention, as in the Haerye account." (Cf. History of the alphabet from Wikipedia)

Western ←		Phoenician	→ Brahmic			→ Korean
Latin	Greek		Gujarati	Devanagari	Tibetan*	
B	B	𐤁	બ	ब	བ	ㅂ, ㅁ
C, G	Γ	𐤂	ગ	ग	ག	ㄱ, (ㆁ)
Z	Z	𐤆	દ (ડ)	द (ड)	ད (ཌ)	ㄷ, ㄴ
L	Λ	𐤋	લ	ल	ལ	ㄹ
-	Ϡ	𐤑	સ	स	ས	ㅈ, ㅅ

Table 1 : The spread of the alphabet west (Greek, Latin) and east (Brahmic, Korean). Note that the exact correspondence between Phoenician (through Aramaic) to Brahmic is uncertain, especially for the sibilants and the letters in parentheses. The transmission of the alphabet from Tibetan (through 'Phags-pa) to Hangeul is also allegedly controversial but unlikely, in particular, from Z to ㄷ, ㄴ. (Cf, History of the alphabet from Wikipedia)

However, this speculation is not true if one read *Hunmin jeong-eum Haerye* without deliberate mal-interpretation. Based on this *Haerye's* explanation that Hangeul had taken the shape of speech organs, it is self-evident that ㄱㄴㅁㅅㅇ are basic. For instance, ㄴ(the shape of tongue-tip touching alveolar ridge) should precede ㄷ in the process of conceiving a series of new letters. If the order would be inverse (which would not be the case though), King Sejong was still a genius phonetician, who showed the shape of tongue-tip touching alveolar ridge very figuratively in his creation of letter shape for alveolar nasal.

ㄷ was an extension from ㄴ by adding a stroke. Sejong had not simply created it ex nihilo but through a systematic extension. Even in Hunmin jeong-eum, ㄷ had a small lip protruding from the upper left corner. This lip indicates the brush-touching trace of an added upper stroke. One should understand this shape ㄷ if he is familiar with East-Asian calligraphy. Therefore, Ledyard (1998) went the wrong direction when forming his argument because he failed to consider the techniques of calligraphy in writing the letter without considering brush-touched tip of the first stroke in ㄷ.

"These were the tenuis(non-voiced, non-aspirated) plosives, g for ㄱ [k], d for ㄷ [t], and b for ㅂ [p], which were basic to Chinese theory, but were not voiced nor considered basic in the Indic languages; as well as the sibilant s for ㅈ [ts] and the liquid l for ㄹ [l].

The non-plosives, nasals ng (see below) ㄴㅁ and the fricative ㅅ, were derived by removing the top of the tenuis letter. (No letters were derived from ㄹ.) This clears up a few points. For example, it's easy to derive ㅁ from ㅂ by removing the top of ㅂ, but it's not clear how you'd get ㅂ by adding something to ㅁ, since ㅂ is not analogous to the other plosive s : if they were derived, as in the traditional account, we'd expect them all to have a similar vertical top stroke." (Cf, History of the alphabet from Wikipedia)

The above statement is an incorrect speculation as I will explain. ㅂ is quite natural extension from ㅁ by adding two stokes in a balanced fashion on both top-corners of square. 'Balance' is underlying orderly baseline of calligraphy. Another balanced shape of two-stroke-added ㅍ will be explained later. Without doubt Sejong started with the shapes of the tongue touching the alveolar and velar region, and the shape of the mouth, which resulted in conceiving the shapes of the letters based on speech organs.

As a result, the King Sejong's court men found that these shapes were somewhat similar to *gǔ zhuān* (Mongol seal script). When it is said in the form of sentence, *zì bang gǔ zhuān*, it literally means "the letter similar to Mongol seal script." Ledyard (1998) mistook this statement to mean 'Phags-pa based on zì bang gǔ zhuān, and did not understand what it really meant. It did not mean "Hangeul was made by imitating Mongol Seal Script" but simply meant "the new alphabet is similar to the shapes of *gǔ zhuān*."

3. The Unique Characteristics of the Korean Alphabet

The unique characteristics of the Korean alphabet are, as mentioned above, 1) the creation of related letters by the addition of strokes to basic letters, and 2) writing words in syllabic units, combining more than two letters within two or three blocks in a square as found in Chinese characters, for example, 珀 or 碧.

However, hangeul also stood in stark contrast with the complex and curvy lines of Chinese characters. No one looking at this original alphabet could fail to differentiate the simplicity. Unlike the letters of other alphabets, hangeul symbols are not written side-by-side on a mono-linear level; rather, the individual letters are arranged into syllabic units. There are typically several different positions where a letter may occur. The shape of vowels may be affected by the presence of glides or final [=coda] consonants, and the shape of consonants by the vowel, the glide, or the presence of final consonants.

When each alphabet is written as an individual letter (combined block of alphabets) in a syllabic unit, there are six syllabic layouts. As illustrated in the following diagram, the individual letters are arranged and proportioned to fit neatly into a square box, and are always read from left to right, and top to bottom. As shown in Table 2, there are several degrees of density in paralleling the strokes : six strokes in the horizontal direction and seven in the vertical direction are the most complex.

빼 : 니　　 를 : 그　　 꿱

vertically dense/sparse　　horizontally dense/sparse　　both, dense

Vowels that are "vertical", like ㅏ, go to the right of the first consonant in a syllable. Vowels that are "horizontal", like ㅗ, go the first consonant in a syllable. All of this is done to make sure that syllables fit in to a square box.

가　　그　　귀　　떡　　굵　　쿤

ㅏ ㅐ	ㅗ	ㅚ ㅘ
ㅑ ㅒ	ㅛ	ㅝ ㅞ
ㅓ ㅔ	ㅜ	ㅢ ㅙ
ㅕ ㅖ	ㅠ	ㅞ
ㅣ	ㅡ	

	Bright Vowel	Dark V.	Neutral V.
Vertically Oriented	ㅏ ㅑ ㅐ ㅒ	ㅓ ㅕ ㅔ ㅖ	ㅣ
Horizontally Oriented	ㅗ ㅛ	ㅜ ㅠ	ㅡ
Mixed-Orientation	ㅘ ㅙ ㅚ	ㅝ ㅞ	ㅢ

Table 2 : How to compose 'Syllabic Units'

The maximal structure of written syllables in Korean is CVCC. While C is optional, V is obligatory. The Korean (written) syllable structure in the formation of letters can therefore be re-written as $(C_1)V(C_2)(C_3)$ but there is a phonological rule of final consonant clusters implification to omit either C_2 or C_3. All the possible combinations of the syllable occurrences are shown below :

V : 아, 와, 왜　　VC : 얼, 움, 은　　VCC : 않, 없, 읋
CV : 가, 보, 뛰　　CVC : 낙, 뿔, 꽝　CVCC : 값, 몫, 뚊

In addition to the characteristics shown at the beginning of Section 3 as Principle 1) and 2), some calligraphic principles are applied as well. The writer must 3) write from left to right, top to bottom, 4) maintain consistency when adding strokes in syllabic units, and 5) limit the size of syllabic units to the inside of squares in equal sequence. All these give a feeling of symmetry and stability, based on geometric and calligraphic beauty (see Table 2).

Each syllable is symmetrical and balanced, much as one would say for Chinese characters. But these are not characters, they are syllables, or perhaps more accurately, morpho-syllables, consisting of alphabetic symbols representing the individual sounds, arranged according to the morphophonological rules involved, such as the rule of the final consonant cluster simplification.

Hangeul can be written both horizontally and vertically. The latter method is traditional, akin to the Chinese style. The former style was promoted since the twentieth century, and has become overwhelmingly preferred. Within each word, syllables are written right next to each other. Between words, however, there are spaces. This way even quickly and messily written hangeul will be legible to Koreans.

Hitherto I explained unquestioned aspects of the Korean writing system including graphemes and calligraphy. Now let us look at other aspects of the system never revealed before.

4. How were the Graphemes of the Korean Alphabet Designed?

The question that has never been asked is *how* King Sejong experimented with various possible strokes and characters on a blank piece of paper. I assume that the king was the initiator of all ideas, since an individual inventor comes up with an embryonic idea at the outset, rather than through brain-storming by a group in creating a new writing system.

In this preliminary stage of creating the Korean written system, it is quite probable that King Sejong used the "trial and error" method, and was not mysteriously inspired by some epiphany which led to a developed idea for the entire set of character. This means Sejong used a brush to draw a draft of scripts for his alphabet. He probably experienced the difficulty of writing dots but decided to stick to using the philosophical symbol of heaven (·). Later, because of their incompatibility with brush strokes and wood carving, these dots were changed to a character that resembled a circle.

4.1. *Economy of Calligraphy*

In the case of ㄱ, ㅋ and ㄴ, the reason why he did not choose ㄷ, ㅌ and ㄴ is that the latter require one more stroke in brush writing. This may be regarded as another calligraphic principle : 6) minimization of strokes. Another interesting example of economy of calligraphy is a change in the shapes of the letters ㅅ, ㅈ, ㅊ with a visible reduction in the number of strokes from original 2, 3, 4 to 1, 2, 3.

4.2. Avoiding Calligraphic Similarity

When King Sejong invented the consonant letters, he may have ended up with several similar characters, as marked by a dotted line in Fig. 2. It is well known that ㅌ and ㄹ printed in small type are often misread even today. Two problem letters were avoided : ㅋ and ㅂ. Thus, 7)calligraphic similarity must be avoided by introducing different shapes.

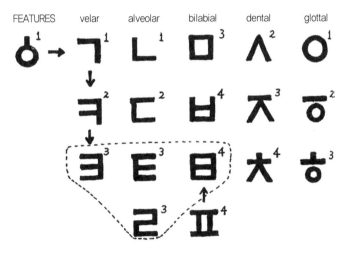

Fig. 2. A Hypothetical and Preliminary Draft for Designing the Korean Alphabet. Cited from Lee, Sang-Oak (1997).

It is my assumption that King Sejong avoided the graphic jam by eliminating ㅋ, shifted ㄱ and ㅋ down to fill a blank, and newly introduced ㆁ as an exceptional measure of avoiding the graphic jam, an interpretation more in line with other ingenious aspects of the Korean Alphabet (Hunmin jeong-eum). As explained above, the script is optimized with maximal distinction in this intricate part of designing the whole alphabet.

Many Korean people generally believe that ㅂ has two additional strokes on the top of ㅁ but it is totally wrong. ㅁ has three strokes and ㅂ simply four in brush writing. So there is not two, but one additional stroke.

As for ㅂ, this shape looks not only like the Chinese character 日 but also like the other Korean letters ㅌ, ㄹ, & ㅋ. Therefore, to avoid this jam in the dotted line of Fig. 1, ㅍ was introduced probably turning ㅐ by 90 degrees. ㅐ is a more natural way of adding strokes to ㅁ & ㅂ, but may have had problems in composing shapes like ㅐㅐ (the first ㅐ as a consonant, the second ㅐ as a vowel).

4.3. More Graphemes with Maximal Distinction

Last but not least, ㅋ was chosen over ㄱ to avoid the probable confusion with ㄷ. ㄱ is one possible way to add a stroke to ㄱ. Likewise, ㅌ is one possible way to add a stroke to ㄴ. It is likely that either the set ㅋ & ㄷ or the set ㄱ & ㅌ would be selected to keep maximal distinction between graphemes as in 7). Avoidance of calligraphic similarity is a general principle of calligraphic distinctiveness.

5. How Convenient Is the Present Assignment of Vowel Shapes?

S. O. Lee (1997) once statistically observed the usage of vertical/horizontal lines in shaping vowel letters of Hunmin-jeongeum. It seems the present choice of assigned lines is very wise distribution considering the frequency of those vowel letters even in terms of modern linguistics. It is also interesting to ask whether King Sejong probably knew that his choice was very wise at that time. He probably choose the shapes of letters under his own decision. [a, ja, ə, jə, i] were assigned to vertical lines while [o, jo, u, ju, ɨ] were to horizontal. The reason why he assigned the first batch to the vertical lines is because they are used more frequently (see Table). When one writes these leters vertically with a brush in the traditional oriental writing more used vowels should be assigned to the set consisting of vertical strokes which makc a long line from the top to the bottom of a 'longitude.'

The Table 2 below shows four kinds of statistics made by three unpublished data and Yu (1985). The first two columns represent pure Korean words and Sino-Korean respectively. The third column shows data in 16-19 centuries and the fourth is pure Korean words in 20th century to refer to the previous data.

	15C.pure Korean		15C.Sino-Korean		Cf. 16~19C. pure Korean		20C.pure Korean	
A. vowel letters with vertical lines								
ㅏ a	4532	14.14%	6252	15.33%	85555	19.93%	28580	24.23%
ㅐ ɛ	922	2.88%	1291	3.17%	7777	1.81%	6171	5.23%
ㅑ ja	548	1.71%	674	1.65%	6957	1.62%	828	0.70%
ㅒ jɛ	26	0.08%	26	0.06%	10	0.002	11	0.009
ㅓ ə	1803	5.62%	2935	7.20%	31995	7.45%	15652	13.27%
ㅔ e	694	2.16%	929	2.28%	11819	2.75%	2208	1.87%
ㅕ jə	1184	3.69%	1817	4.46%	33743	7.86%	2466	2.09%
ㅖ je	359	1.12%	426	1.04%	3825	0.89%	185	0.16%
ㅣ I	7043	21.97%	8200	20.11%	63103	14.70%	21785	18.47%
·ㅣ ʌi	730	2.28%	730	1.79%	10762	2.51%	—	—
소 계		55.65%		57.09%		59.52%		66.03%
B. vowel letters with vertical lines								
ㅜ u	3612	11.27%	4669	11.45%	53392	12.44%	11413	9.68%
ㅗ o	221	0.69%	368	0.90%	5696	1.33%	314	0.27%
ㅛ jo	1015	3.17%	2096	5.14%	31251	7.28%	14189	12.03%
ㅠ ju	77	0.24%	186	0.46%	6957	1.62%	155	0.13%
— i	2520	7.86%	2806	6.88%	33795	7.87%	10299	8.73%
· ʌ	5582	17.41%	5585	13.70%	18064	4.21%	—	—
소 계		40.64%		38.53%		34.75%		30.84%
C. vowels of vertical/horizontal lines								
ㅘ wa	302	0.94%	567	1.39%	7889	1.84%	718	0.61%
ㅙ wɛ	45	0.14%	51	0.13%	231	0.05%	200	0.17%
ㅚ Ø	274	0.85%	340	0.83%	2946	0.69%	899	0.76%
ㅝ wə	56	0.17%	131	0.32%	3092	0.72%	246	0.21%
ㅞ we	6	0.02%	6	0.01%	86	0.02%	74	0.06%
ㅟ y	154	0.48%	272	0.67%	2993	0.70%	1304	1.11%
ㅢ ii	355	1.11%	422	1.03%	7359	1.71%	233	0.20%
소 계		3.71%		4.38%		5.78%		3.13%
총 계		100%		100%		100%		100%

Table 2. Frequencies of vowel letters in three different periods

As attested in 〈Table 2〉 A-group vowel with a vertical

pole occurs more frequent than B-group vowel with a horizontal beam. If they were inverted, that is, ㅏ to [o] and ㅗ to [a] and so on, then brush writing might be awkward and ineffective.

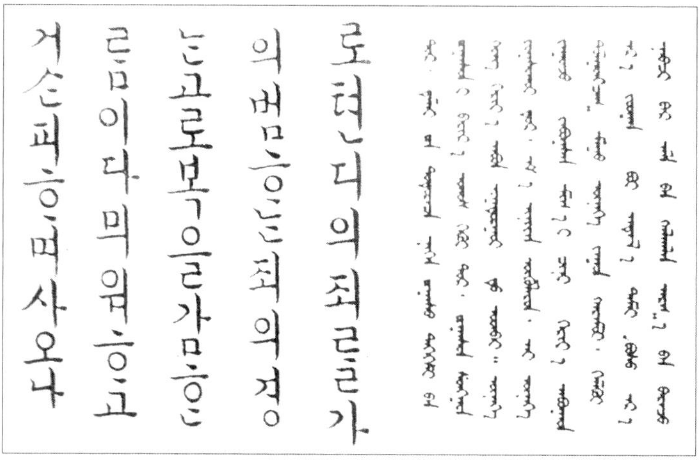

Picture 3. 'Palace style' (left) and Mongolian style

As shown in 〈Picture 3〉 both Korean (so-called 'Palace style') and Mongolian style use the vertical pole. No matter thatSejong relates frequency of vowels to the vertical sroke or not, the present assignment has entailed great benefit to calligraphers and ordinary people. Maybe the inverse assignment is desirable in the modernized writing style on horizontal lines like English. However, even in horizontal writing including Western (like English) penmanship we use more vertical line as confirmed in 〈Picture 4〉.

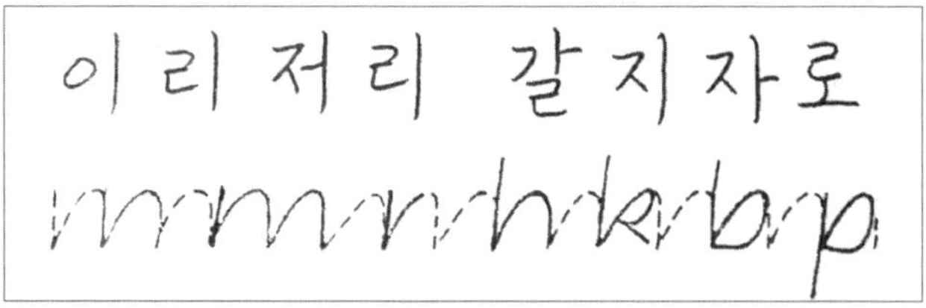

Picture 4. Korean horizontal writing and English penmanship

Although English penmanship is horizontal writing, one usually uses all three fingers (thumb, index and middle fingers together) 'vertilly' rather than horizontally.

6. An Optimal Featural System

De Francis (1989) claims that Bell's "Visible Speech (VS)" is featural because it consistently takes a C-shaped symbol for *consonant*. However, C-shape has <u>any</u> figurative similarity like ㄱ -shape for the tongue touching the velar. One cannot justify why C should be used as a feature for consonants. It could be K in many languages such as German. In early Roman alphabet, C represented both the hard 'k' sound in 'cat' and the 'g' sound in 'garden'. gaml "throwstick" is regarded as the origin of ΓCG but it never shows any association to 'consonants' *per se*.

Consonants in VS are x-high : they define the "normal" height of letters by not ascending higher than it, nor do they descend below the baseline. The basic forms are based on curves representing the four main places of articulation : the back of the tongue, the top of the tongue, the tip of the tongue, and the lips. (Cf. http://web.meson.org/write/vs- overview.php)

C   ∩   ʊ   ɔ

Back (of tongue). Top (of tongue). Point (of tongue). Lip.

All scripts developed from the base of C have no physiological ground of being assimilated to the speech organs. Using C as a base may be an artificial marker but not natural and universally applicable feature. What is really "visible" in Visible Speech? Similar looking symbols with almost undistinguishable variations from C.

(Non-Vocal)   Ɔ Ɔ Ɛ Ʊ ∪ ω ʊ ʊ Ω ∩ ɑ
             p wh f t rh lh s th sh yh k

(Vocal)   Ɛ Ɛ Ɛ Ʊ ω ω ʊ ʊ Ω ω ɛ
            b w v d r l z dh zh y g

As a result, this *consistent* iconic alphabet ends up with shapes that prove equivocally confusing for laymen with so many similar C-shapes and cannot be used as a universal phonetic writing system in any practical case. In VS C stands for all consonantal and ɑ is k with velar closure which represents a sort of feature, while In Hangeul ㄱ shows velar closure directly. Although VS was a naïve featural script, Bell failed to understand where to leave this naivety. But King Sejong, the creator of the first version of Korean alphabet, knew how to make a featural system more practical. Sejong's solution of the adding a stroke to ㄱ to graphically represent aspirated ㅋ is easy, distinctive, and legible. The Hangeul convention seems more natural and easy to master compared to its equivalent, VS.

It is notable that these are all full-fledged spacing characters in VS, whereas in IPA many of these functions are handled by combining characters. This is again due (presumably) to considerations of economy : Even with computers, typesetting diacritics is more difficult than stringing spacing characters together. Sweet messed with the representation of a few of these, which he feared were hard to distinguish, but most of them remain. (Cf. http://web.meson.org/write/vs-overview.php)

Sproat (2000) classified Hangeul as "an intelligently constructed segmental alphabet." However, speaking beyond taxanomic nomenclature, I believe that Hangeul is not just another intelligently constructed featural alphabet, but the **optimal featural system**. It is more than a segmental system that qualifies as a featural system but wisely avoids becoming completely featural by allowing a variation like ㅍ. As I explained above, King Sejong had "a tight spatiogeometrical constraint of having to represent characters in mutually distinctive shapes, each with no more than a few strokes."(Kim 1997)

In addition, the Korean vowel script retains more vertical strokes for the statistically frequent vowel group (cf. Lee, Sang-Oak, 1997) because it is easier to move our fingers and hand vertically well with a brush. I believe Sejong, as a born linguist was surely aware of relationships such as the one between the frequency of sounds and the assignment of vertical strokes, and used this awareness to create the most optimal featural writing system.

❖ References

Coulmas, Florian(1989), *The Writing Systems of the World*. Cambridge, MA : Basil Blackwell Inc.

Coulmas, Florian(1996), *The Blackwell Encyclopedia of Writing Systems*. Oxford : Blackwell.

Coulmas, Florian(2003), *Writing Systems : An Introduction to their Linguistic Analysis*. Cambridge : Cambridge University Press.

Daniels, Peter T. and William Bright, eds.(1996), *The World's Writing Systems*. Oxford : Oxford University Press.

DeFrancis, John(1984), *The Chinese Language : Fact and Fantasy*. Honolulu : University of Hawaii Press.

DeFrancis, John(1989), *Visible Speech : The Diverse Oneness of Writing Systems*, Honolulu : Univ. of Hawai'i Press.

Gelb, I.J.(1963), *A Study of Writing.* London, (2 ed.)

Kim, Chin-Woo(1997), "The structure of phonological units in Han'gul," in Young-Key Kim-Reanud, ed. (1997) 145-160.

Kim, Wanjin(1975), Hunmin Chong'um chaumja-wa kahoek-uy wolli (The consonant letters in *Hunmin Chong'um* and the principle of adding strokes) , *Omunyon'gu* 7 & 8, also in Lee Ki-Moon ed. (1977), 217-27.

Kim-Reanud, Young-Key ed.(1997), *The Korean Alphabet : Its History and Structure.* Honolulu : Univ. of Hawai'i Press.

Ledyard, Gari K.(1998), *The Korean Language Reform of 1446.* Seoul : Shingu munhwasa.

Lee, Ki-Moon ed.(1977), *Muntcha* (Scripts), *Kugohak Nonmunson* (Selected Papers in Korean Linguistics) 7, Seoul : Minjungseogwan.

Lee, Ki-Moon(1992), *Hunmin jeong-eum chinjeron* (The evidences for none but King Sejong's invention of *Hunmin jeong-eum*), *Hangukmunhwa* 13.

Lee, Sang-Oak(1997), "Graphical ingenuity in the Korean writing system : With new reference to calligraphy," in Young-Key Kim-Reanud, ed. (1997) 107-116.

Lee, Sang-Oak(2008), Understanding *Hunmin jeong-eum.* Seoul : National Language Institute.

Rogers, Henry(2005), *Writing systems : A linguistic approach.* Malden, MA : Blackwell Publishing.

Sampson, Geoffrey(1985), *Writing systems.* Stanford, CA : Stanford University Press.

Sisayongosa ed.(1983), *The Korean Language.* Seoul : Sisayongosa.

Sproat, Richard(2000), *A Computational Theory of Writing Systems*, Cambridge : Cambridge University Press.

Taylor, Insup & M. Martin Taylor(1995), *Writing and Literacy in Chinese, Korean, and Japanese.* Amsterdam : John Benjamins.

Yu, Jae-Won(1985), *Korean Reverse Dictionary,* Jeongeum-sa.

web.meson.org/write/vs-overview.php

Wikipedia, History of the alphabet.

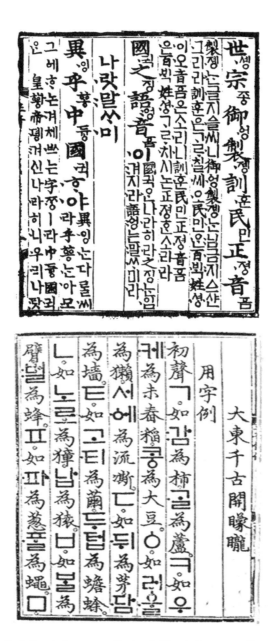

The faximilied *Hunmin jeong-eum Eonhae* & *Hunmin jeong-eum Haerye* (below)

○

Not Copy but Envy
The Korean Alphabet Did not Imitate Mongol 'Phags-pa but Was Invented with Graphical Originality*

Summary : One cannot, on the basis of mere six instances of unsystematic 'similarities,' make a claim that the Korean alphabet was created by 'copying' from Chinese characters. Nor can one come to a conclusion that the Korean Hangeul is a 'copy' or an 'imitation' of 'Phags-pa just because there appears to be five characters that are accidentally similar in shape and sound value.

One can only be puzzled by the motives behind the failure to give credit where credit is due. The formation of the basic Hangeul characters on the featural basis of the speech organs and the creation of the other characters through systematic addition of strokes to mark phonetic features clearly reveal the

---

* Inquiries into Korean Linguistics IV, 2011, 143-164.

ingenuity and the creative genius of King Sejong.

In searching for a reasonable explanation for why some scholars conclude Hangeul is a work of 'imitation' and not 'invention,' one is almost led to wonder if it is not a simple case of 'Hangeul Envy.'

1. 'Phags-pa Script as a Possible Model for the Korean Consonants?

Some scholars have posed the writing systems of neighboring countries as possible sources of imitation for Hangeul. Ledyard (1966) and Yu Chang-gyun (1966) suggested the 'Phags-pa script as a possible model for the Korean alphabet, pointing in particular to the 'Phags-pa consonants ᠊[d] and ᠊[l] for Korean ㄷ[t] and ㄹ[l]. However, they failed to address the issue of the fact that the other letter shapes, like Korean ㄹ[l], ㅅ[s], ㅈ [č], and ㅌ[t'], do not have the same sound values as the similar 'Phags-pa letters ㄹ[ŋ], ㅅ[o], ㅈ[o], and ㅌ[j]. Based on what can only be regarded as coincidental similarities, it is difficult to justify a claim of 'systematic correspondence.' (Lee Sang-Oak 1997) In particular, 'Phags-pa consonants ᠊[g] and ᠊[b] are quite different from Korean ㄱ[k] and ㅂ[p] in their system.

Let us briefly introduce the hypothesis of the 'Phags-pa script as a model for the Korean alphabet. Ledyard (1966) suggests that the core consonants of Hangeul were based on the 'Phags-pa script, with the other consonants derived from Aramaic abjad or Proto-Sinaitic. (Cf. History of the alphabet from Wikipedia) Ledyard suggests that portions of Hangeul's consonantal system may be based on half a dozen letters derived from the 'Phags-pa script (1269?-1360) of the Yuan dynasty of China known as the mĕnggŭzhuānzì (蒙古篆字 Mongol seal script).

Western ←		Phoenician	→ Brahmic			→ Korean
Latin	Greek		Gujarati	Devanagari	Tibetan*	
B	B	𐤁	બ	ब	བ	ㅂ, ㅁ
C, G	Γ	𐤂	ગ	ग	ག	ㄱ, (ㆁ)
Z	Z	𐤆	દ (ડ)	द (ड)	ད (ཌ)	ㄷ, ㄴ
L	Λ	𐤋	લ	ल	ལ	ㄹ
-	ϡ	𐤔	સ	स	ས	ㅈ, ㅅ

*Tibetan(7c.AD) alphabets are used here in place of 'Phags-pa(13c.AD) because of font availability in HWP.

Table 1 : The spread of the alphabet west (Greek, Latin) and east (Brahmic, Korean). Note that the exact correspondence between Phoenician (through Aramaic) to Brahmic is uncertain, especially for the sibilants and the letters in parentheses. The transmission of the alphabet from Tibetan (through 'Phags-pa) to Hangeul is unlikely given the differences Z to ㄷ, ㄴ. (Cf. History of the alphabet from Wikipedia)

Let us first look at the views of Ledyard(1966). (cf.

"History of the alphabet from Wikipedia")

"Only five letters were adopted from ' Phags-pa, with most of the rest of the consonants created by featural derivation from these, as described in the account in the Hunminjeong-eum Haerye. However, the two accounts differ as to which letters were the basic consonants.

Whereas the Haerye implies that the graphically simplest letters ㄱ ㄴ ㅁ ㅅ ㅇ are basic, with the others derived from them by the addition of strokes (though with ㆁㄹㅿ set apart), Ledyard believes the five phonologically simplest letters ㄱㄷㄹㅂ ㅈ, which were basic in Chinese phonology, were the basic letters of Hangeul. Other characters being derived by the addition or subtraction of strokes to these basic letters. In his account, it was these five core letters which were taken from the ' Phags-pa script, and ultimately derive from the letters ꡂ ꡊ[1] ꡙ ꡎ ꡛ. Thus, according to his account, they may be cognate with Greek letters Γ Δ Λ B and the Latin letters C/G D L B. The sixth basic letter, ㅇ, was an invention, as in the Haerye account."

To ask us to accept that the letters whose forms match exactly the shapes of the speech organs in the production of

---

1) For the Korean ㄹ, Ledyard's choice of ꡙ[l] is awkward as the 'Phags-pa ㄹ [ng] is manifestly a closer match for the Korean ㄹ. Likewise, ꡛ[s] for the Korean ㅈ is deliberate as the 'Phags-pa ㅈ[o] is figuratively closer to the Korean ㅈ. He intentionally inclined to match sounds than graphs.

those very sounds, that is the letters ㅁ, ㄴ, ㅅ(m, n, s), were derived by King Sejong by systematically removing the strokes from the letters, so the "copy" argument goes, based on 'Phags-pa letters, namely the letters ㅂ, ㄷ, ㅈ, surely amounts to asking us to accept a quite remarkable "coincidence of improbable."

Table 2 : From en:Image:Phags-pa-Hangeul_comparison.png : (Top) The 'Phags-pa letters [k, t, p, s, l], and their Hangeul derivatives, g, t, b, j, l [k, t, p, ts, l]. Note the lip on both [t]'s. (Middle) The derivation of 'Phags-pa w, v, f from variants of the letter. (Bottom) The derivation of 'Phags-pa ka, kha, ga, nga from variants of the letter.

Who could have possibly known that by starting with the

shapes similar to existing three letters in 'Phags-pa, and by removing the strokes from these letters, that one would end up with exactly the shapes of the speech organs in the production of the sounds indicated by the derived letters? Even this author, who believes King Sejong to have shown himself a genius in creating Hangeul, must hesitate from crediting him with such improbable foresight.

It would be far more reasonable, and certainly more in accord with common sense, to start with the letters in the shape of the speech organs in the production of the sounds represented by those letters, once again ㅁ, ㄴ, ㅅ (m, n, s), and then derive the next series of letters by the addition of strokes, ending with ㅂ, ㄷ, ㅈ.

It is surely sophistry to ask us to accept a derivation based on "coincidence of improbable" over the derivation that seems natural and reasonable. The author of this paper has to wonder, at a loss for any way of explaining the cause for such sophistry, that perhaps envy is the cause.

However, without what can only amount to an intentional mis-interpretation or a mis-reading of *Hunminjeong-eum Haerye*, one cannot come to such conclusions as above. First, *Haerye*'s explanation is clear that Hangeul was based on the shape of the speech organs, and that ㄱㄴㅁㅅㅇ are clearly identified as the basic letters. For instance, ㄴ (the shape of tongue-tip touching the alveolar ridge) should precede ㄷ in the process of creating a series of new letters. Even if the order were reversed (this was not the case though), King Sejong revealed his phonetic insight and inspired creativity in his creation of the letter-form that 'pictures' a snapshot of the tongue-tip touching the alveolar ridge in the process of producing the alveolar nasal 'n.'

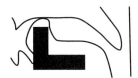

And as the derivation of ㄷ(d) as an extension from ㄴ (n) by the addition of a stroke shows, King Sejong applied systematic rules of extensions to create the other letters and not ex *nihilo*.

At this point, I would like to raise the issue of the important role that calligraphic principles play in East-Asia. Given the special and important place that calligraphy and the brush has in the East-Asian culture, I believe we risk mistakes and misinterpretations, even in modern linguistic analysis, if we fail to consider the calligraphic principles that loom large in our analysis. I believe the failure to consider the calligraphic principles at play has been particularly detrimental in the analysis of the Hangeul. This can be seen in Ledyard's account of the basic letters and the derivation process of Hangeul.

As a case in point, it is an often missed feature, but in *Hunminjeong-eum*, ㄷ had a small lip protruding beyond the upper-left corner. This lip indicates the brush-touching trace of an added upper stroke. Those familiar with East-Asian calligraphy would easily recognize and understand the ㄷ shape. As I will argue, Ledyard (1998) was misled in forming his argument because he failed to take into consideration the calligraphic principles at work in the formation of the letter ㄷ, with the brush-touched tip of the first stroke in ᢛ of 'Phags-pa.

Following is the account of the basic and the derived letters according to Ledyard which I will explore further :
"These were the (non-voiced, non-aspirated) plosives, g for ㄱ [k], d for ㄷ [t], and b for ㅂ [p], which were basic to Chinese theory, but were not voiced nor considered basic in the Indic languages; as well as the sibilant s for ㅈ [ts] and the liquid l for ㄹ [l].

The non-plosives, nasals ng (see below) ㄴㅁ and the fricative ㅅ, were derived by removing the top of the tenuis letter. (No letters were derived from ㄹ.) This clears up a few points. For example, it is easy to derive ㅁ from ㅂ by removing the top of ㅂ, but it's not clear how to get ㅂ by adding something to ㅁ, since ㅂ is not analogous to the other plosive s : if they were derived, as in the traditional account, we would expect them all to have a similar vertical top stroke." (Cf, History of the alphabet from Wikipedia)

First, the above account of the derivation of ㅁ from ㅂ is at best speculative. Further, if one applies the calligraphic principle of balance, ㅂ is found to be a natural extension from ㅁ through the addition of the two strokes to the top-corners of the square. 'Balance,' one of the basic principles of calligraphy, is being forgotten in the above account. Another balanced shape is two-stroke-added ㅍ.

Without a doubt, King Sejong started with the letters in imitation of the shapes of the tongue touching the alveolar and the velar region, and the shape of the mouth, which makes clear how the Korean alphabets mirror the organs of human speech in action.

Now, we must address the issue of 'imitation' and 'invention.' While 'imitation' would frequently lead to 'invention', it would appear that a statement to the affect that a part of Hangeul "was made in imitation of the Chinese (not Mongol) seal script" was misinterpreted by some scholars like Ledyard and Yu Chang-gyun to mean that Hangeul "was invented in imitation' of the Mongol seal script." As will be presented below, such interpretation is unwarranted and ultimately untenable.

In commenting on Hangeul, the members of the court of King Sejong noted that the shapes of some of the letters were 'similar' to gǔzhuān (古篆 old seal script). It is only natural that the 'new' characters were likened to what were already 'familiar.'

But the exact statement of similarities between Hangeul and gǔzhuān was the following : "zìbanggǔzhuān"(字倣古篆), which literally means "the letters were made in imitation of the old Seal script." But the letters were invented by mirroring the organs of speech. And, in as much as the newly created Hangeul was a phonetic alphabet (in their initial and final consonants, and vowels), just as was the old seal script, the observant courtiers may have been noting this fact even more than some coincidental similarity in shape between the two character sets. Ledyard (1997) however mistook this statement of "zìbanggǔzhuān" to mean that "Hangeul was made by imitating the Mongol Seal script" with only imaginary interpretation.

For several reasons as expanded on below, the semi-literal interpretation of '象形而字倣古篆' as '(Hunminjeong-eum) being modeled after the shape of the speech organs, in consequence, they appear to have been modeled on the ancient Chinese characters'2) is far more plausible than any 'Phags-pa origin hypothesis.

1) Given the then recently emergent hegemony of Ming China, it seems reasonable that King Sejong's own nation-building strategy and political considerations might have led him to desire to link Hunminjeong-eum's origin to the Chinese characters, thereby achieving both legitimacy and authority for Hunminjeong-eum, none of which would have been achieved had he linked his work to the script of the fallen and disgraced Mongol dynasty.

2) Had he desired to link the Hunminjeong-eum's origin to Chinese characters to appease and satisfy the powerful pro-Ming faction, his goal would have been best achieved by emphasizing the likeness of Hunminjeong-eum to the most ancient of the Chinese characters, the 古篆, (cf. Ahn, 2007, p.68, fn.19). It is perhaps in this political context that "倣古篆" statement should be understood.

3) Composing the syllable within the confine of a square is also a feature more clearly evident in the more familiar

---

2) Incidentally, Albrecht Huwe (2010) presented a quite agreeable interpretation : "while forming the shapes the letters imitate [the principle] of the old seal script." He could not attend the 17th International Conference on Korean Linguistics (July 6–8, Ulaanbataar) but submitted a draft. The author also presented the same view in this conference and we agree gǔzhuān is not the Mongol seal script but the old Chinese seal script.

Chinese characters (each read as a syllable within a square), and one need not seek a model for this in the actually less known and less familiar 'Phags-pa script which also shares this feature. Looked at this way, if we also take into consideration the fact that 'Phags-pa is also written vertically (in contrast to the pan-Indic horizontal tradition) and that it is syllabic, 'Phags-pa script shows clear evidence of being modeled on and of emulating the "Chinese" writing system.

4) Further, the design of shapes and stroke order of Hunminjeong-eum syllables show that much consideration was given for harmonization with Chinese characters. Given such observations, it would be far more reasonable to look to the familiar and at-hand Chinese characters for the explanation of the origin of Hangeul than to look to the less familiar and far more distant 'Phags-pa origin hypothesis.

Above observations will be further developed in the second part of this work along with data showing that, in a global script comparison, Chinese characters are found to have the highest number of matching basic strokes when compared to Hangeul.

The above observations are offered more to put to rest the 'Phags-pa origin hypothesis than to suggest some Chinese character origin hypothesis. Rather, this work would like to present a complete reassessment of "similar therefore copied from original" arguments as applied to Hunminjeong-eum.

It is only natural that Hangeul has similarities with Hanja. Before the invention of Hangeul, Hanja was the script we had used for over 1,500 years. It would be far stranger for Hangeul not to have been influenced by the writing system that Koreans had both known so intimately and used for so long.

In consequence, Hangeul's composition structure, figuration within a well defined square, and the ability to write both horizontally and vertically are well reflected in the outstanding design features that achieve harmony in common use with Chinese character.

And as the many Korean translation of Chinese texts (諺解本) published in the early years of Hangeul advocacy show, the clear premise was that Hanja and Hangeul were to be used harmoniously together. The wisdom evident in harmonizing two writing systems is one that still calls forth both admiration and a sense of marvel. This fact can be observed by contrasting the sense of "foreignness" that is unavoidable when Hangeul and Roman alphabet is used together.[3]

---

3) Of course, Koreans had also developed Idu, based on Chinese characters, which was used interlinearly with Chinese characters. However, by design criteria, Idu failed to fit harmoniously with the Chinese characters. On the

Were one to posit a hypothesis that Hangeul was modeled on Hanja because they have in common 6 basic strokes, such would be at best a hypothesis built on scattering clouds. First, one can not find any sound correspondence in any of the shape correspondences. And similarly numerous shape likeness can be found with other characters or with other script systems. The situation is quite simply identical to the shaky argument that Phags-pa is the model for Hangeul. Just as Phags-pa hypothesis is disingenuous at best, this Hanja-hypothesis can not but be disingenuous at best.

Ultimately raising of Hanja model hypothesis, indeed any x-model hypothesis, does not mean at all that another challenge to the uniqueness and originality of Hangeul has been newly posed. Rather, the author wishes that this work will go some way in pointing out the disingenuousness and the logical weakness of all such x-model hypothesis in the case of

---

other hand, Hangeul is the result of a comprehensive scientific phonetic analysis with superb graphic design.

Here, Hangeul, successfully isolating vowels from consonants unlike other Asian scripts, the vowels and consonants are fully distinguished and each syllable is systematically visualized within the square with syllable consonants (including null) graphically describing the speech organs in the production of each sound and taking the central position and the vowels positioned according to physical phonetic criterion, below the consonant for central and round vowels (ㅗㅜㅡ)and to the right of the consonant for other vowels (ㅏㅓㅣ). In these respects, Korean Idu and Japanese kana, both derived from Chinese characters, are fundamentally different from in nature from the analytic and visual Hangeul.

Hunminjeong-eum.

"Ledyard argues this largely by interpreting a remark in the Hunminjeong-eum as a deliberately cryptic reference to Mongolian writing, and this argument seems contrived. It may well be true that Sejong knew of 'Phags-pa and other phonographic scripts in use in East Asia, but those scripts were all segmental : they offer no precedent for Han'gul." (cf. 'Phags-pa script, from Wikipedia)

Because Professor Ledyard wrote at length on the Phags-pa origin of Hangeul hypothesis in his thesis, even while expressing clear agreement, in the same publication, with the view that Hangeul was based on the shapes of the speech organs, he has ever since come to be seen as the representative proponent of the 'Phags-pa origin hypothesis.

Faced with this odd contradiction of clear agreement with the speech organ model view appearing side by side with the lengthy exposition on the 'Phags-pa origin hypothesis, this author, at a loss for any other explanation, is led to the unavoidable conclusion that "envy" may be the psychological explanation for why these two contradictory views are found together in Prof. Ledyard's writing.

It seems that he does not advocate two origins at the same time, although someone may take that kind of ambiguous position. So far, nobody has provided an objectively acceptable proof of the Phags-pa origin hypothesis.

2. Hangeul in the Context of Other World Scripts : Within the Set of Typical Strokes Frequently Used in any Alphabet

Within the context of any writing system, given that the number of elementary strokes are rather limited, being either vertical, horizontal, and slanted lines; triangles, circles and variously oriented curves frequently used in alphabets.[4] cf. S.-O. Lee 1997:107 & also Dürscheid 2006:87-88.[5] It should be no surprise some subset of one writing system is found to be 'similar' to some other subset of another writing system. Even the

---

4) Strikingly similar ideas can also be found in the works of Cheng Ch'iao (鄭樵 1104~1162) in his 六書略 (A Summary of Six Letter Types) in 通志 Vol. 34 where through his 起一成文圖 (Illustration of creating all the letter starting with 一 /Generation of Letter from the One Stroke) he associated 衡, 從, 邪, 反, 折, 轉, 側, 方, 圓, 偶, with the following basic geometric elements 一, |, /, \, ㄱ,ㄷ,ㄴ,ㄴ,ㅅ,ㄴ,Ⅴ,<,>,ㄇ,ㄴ,ㄷ, ㄱ,ㅁ,○, ●, (but no △), etc.

5) Dürscheid (2006) also agrees that the hypotheses against invention has not been proven, quoting instead my position (Lee 1997) that "these similarities are the result of the limited number of the set of strokes (vertical, horizontal, and slanted lines, and circles)."

above mentioned basic strokes would be ready candidates for 'similarity' without there ever being any 'imitation.'

I would like to explore the 'similarity' issue in the broader context of world writing systems by looking at the similarities between Hangeul and the other major writing systems like Minoan, Phoenician, Greek, Hebrew, Brahmi, Roman, Cyrillic, Chinese and Japanese.

Below are the visual similarities that can be found between Hangeul and the other writing systems. Here, to increase the number of correspondences, visual similarity is given priority and sound correspondences are often ignored. [○14, ㄴ13, ㅅ13, ㄱ11 and △11 are frequent in visual similarity among graphic shapes shared with Hangeul.]

Hangeul 1443/ total	○ 14	ㄱ 11	ㅋ 2	ㄴ 13	ㄷ 7	ㅌ 8	ㄹ 1	ㅁ 6	ㅂ 0	ㅅ 13	▲ 11	ㅈ 2
Hiero-glyphic 30cBC 1								$\frac{\square}{[p]}$				
Minoan 30cBC 3	$\frac{O}{[a]}$			$\frac{\llcorner}{[li]}$							$\frac{\triangle}{[ya]}$	
Phoenician 15cBC 3	$\frac{\circ}{[o]}$			$\frac{\vee}{[l]}$		$\frac{\exists}{[e]}$					$\frac{\triangle}{[d]}$	
Ethiopian 8cBC 2		$\frac{\Lambda}{[g]}$			$\frac{C}{[r]}$					$\frac{\Lambda}{[l]}$		
Greek -7cBC- 6	$\frac{O}{[ʕ]}$	$\frac{\daleth}{[p]}$ EarlyG		$\frac{\vee}{[l]}$ EarlyG		$\frac{E}{[e]}$ ModG				$\frac{\Lambda[c,}{g, l]}$ Early, ModG	$\frac{\triangle}{[d]}$	

	ㅇ	ㄱ	ㅋ	ㄴ	ㄷ	ㅌ	ㄹ	ㅁ	ㅂ	ㅅ	ㅿ	ㅈ
Hebrew 6cBC 3	oᗡ [s]	ㄱㄱ [d]						ㅁᗞ [m]				
cf.Arabic numerals	○ 5	ㄱ 6								ㅅ 8		
Brahmi 3cBC 6	O [th]	(ㄱ6) [ʋ])	(ㅋ [th])	ㄴ [u]	ㄷ [n]			ㅁ [b]		∧ [g]	△ [e]	
Berber 2cBC 4	O [r]				ㄷ [d]	(ㅌ7) [t])		ㅁ [r]		∧ [g]		
Iberian 2cBC 3								ㅁ [p]		∧ [l]	△ [t]	
Sassanide 3cAD- 2		ㄱ [r]			ㄷ [t]							
Carian ca.5cAD 4	○ [o]					E [u]		ㅁ [e]			△ [l]	
Roman -6cAD- 2	O [o]				C	E [e]						
Cyrillic 9cAD 4	O [o]				C	E [e]				Λ, Л [l]	△ Д [d]	
Yezidi 14cAD 5	O [h]	ㄱ [t]		ㄴ [m]				ㅁ [d]			△ [g]	
Chinese 14cBC 7		ㄟᄀ Pinyin b	ㅋ tiao	ㄴyin (=隱)	ㄷfang Pinyin f	巴	己 chi	ㅁ kou		人ren jen		大
Japanese 8cAD 5		ヲ [fu]	ㅋ [o]	レ [re]	ヒ [hi]	モ [mo]		ㅁ [ro]		へ [he]		ス [su]
Korean Idu, 6cAD 4		ㄱ [ya]		レ [sa]	ㄷ [ni]		弖 [i]	ㅁ [ko, ku]		ㅅ[tʌ], 八[k], [yə]		ス [myə]
Willis 1602 4	O TH	ㄱ D		L F	⊆ T					∧ A		
Cherokee 1821 3				**L** [tle]		**E** [kə]				**Λ** [ne]		

6) ㄱ and ㅋ are found in Kharosthi which is older and more local than Brahmi. This script was used in the Emperor Mauryan's inscription in the old

	ㅇ	ㄱ	ㅋ	ㄴ	ㄷ	ㅌ	ㄹ	ㅁ	ㅂ	ㅅ	ㅿ	ㅈ
Cree 1840 5		ꞁ [me]		L [ma]		Ɛ [kə]				Λ [pi]	Δ [i]	
Fraser 1915 5	O [o]	ꞁ [ɯ]		L [l]		E [e]				Λ [ng]		
Pollard 1936 6	O [o]	ꞁ [h]		L [l]	ᄃ [tɕ]					Λ [z, y]	Δ [tl]	
' Phagspa, 1243 1	○	ㄱ ᠊ [g]	ㅋ	ㄴ	᠊[d], cf.᠊[n]	cf.ᠷ [dʑ]	᠊ [l] cf.ㄹ [ng]	᠊[b]	ㅂ ᠊ b	人 cf./\ [o] not initial	Δ	ㅈ ᠊ [s] cf.ㅈ [o]

Table 3 : Comparison of similarities of the strokes in many alphabets

Those underlined (in Table 3) are closer to the Korean alphabet than other candidates. Their matching numbers are as follows :

1 : Hieroglyphic, 'Phags-pa

2 : Roman, Ethiopian, Sassanide (Pehlevi),[8]

3 : Minoan (or Crete, Cypriote), Phoenician, Hebrew, Iberian (Proto-Hispanic), *Cherokee*[9]

4 : Korean Idu, Cyrillic, Carian (Anatolian),[10] Berber (including

---

Ashoka. Rogers(2005) p.205, Daniels and Bright(1996) pp.373~383.

7) Tifinigh which is modern Tuareg has E [t] which was not existed in old Berber scripts. Daniels and Bright(1996) p.114.

8) The Sassanides Dynasty(226~651) in the north of Iran used a kind of the Pehlevi alphabet. Février(1995) pp.295, 316.

9) All Italicized names of scripts like Cherokee, Cree, Frazer, Pollard and *Willis's* stenographic device were introduced after the invention of Hangeul in 1443.

10) Carian inscriptions have been found in southwestern Asia Minor and in

Libyan), *Willis*[11]

5 : Japanese Kana, Yezidi (Balti),[12] *Cree*,[13] *Fraser*[14]

6 : Chinese Hanja (including Pinyin[15]), Greek, Brahmi, *Pollard*[16]

If one applies the stricter criteria for "matching" as applied in the above table, there is only one closer form to be found in 'Phags-pa : ㄷ. The 'Phags-pa ㄹ[ng] is clearly a better match than ㄽ[l] for the Korean ㄹ. Even granting that Ledyard's choice of ㄽ[l] over ㄹ[ng] was dictated by the constraint of sound correspondence, the very superiority of the match of ㄹ[ng] to Korean f in their shapes has to be seen as weakening Ledyard's own argument. Note Brahmi as in Table 1 originated from Phoenician shares six matchings, while (Tibetan and) 'Phags-pa

---

Egypt and written during the first millennium. Daniels and Bright(1996) pp.281, 285.

11) John Willis made the first phonetically grounded shorthand system in 1602. Daniels and Bright(1996) p.810.

12) The Yezidi cryptic alphabet is a script used in Baltistan, Kashmir. Diringer (1996) p.299.

13) *Inuktitut syllabic* also shows the same matching shapes as Cree. Missionaries introduced syllabics to Inuit Eskimo in 1856. Likewise *Chipewyan sylllabary* in 1870. Daniels and Bright(1996) pp.599~611.

14) J. O. Fraser, a missionary in China, created an Indic-style script using the Roman capital letters for the Tibetan-Burman language Lisu in about 1915.

15) Pinyin (Chinese : 拼音 : pīnyīn), or more formally Hanyu Pinyin (漢語拼音 / 漢語拼音), is currently the most commonly used romanization system for Standard Mandarin since 1958.

16) S. Pollard, a missionary in China, devised a script comprising geometric symbols for the Miao people, whose language is Western Hmong and proposed improvements by 1936.

shows only one matiching.

Among above statistics, only from 4 to 6, Korean Idu, Japanese Kana and Chinese Hanja are found to be significant. As the above data show, Idu, Kana and Hanja (Kanji) are the most likely candidates of influence, if any, for the Korean alphabet, with the interesting fact that the Chinese characters offer up more striking correspondences than the Korean Idu. We also find that the Greek alphabet and the Cyrillic letters show many notable similarities, something not unsurprising inasmuch as the inventors, the Cyril brothers, modeled the new letters on the Greek alphabet.

It should also be pointed out that the Korean alphabet shares significantly more matching shapes with the Greek alphabet than with Idu or Kana, all scripts of immediate geographic vicinity. And if we were to follow "many similar shapes, therefore a copy" line of argument, we are forced to the rather untenable conclusion that the Korean alphabet most likely was modeled on or copied the Greek alphabet, despite the fact that the Greek cultural sphere is the one geographically most remote amongst the possible candidates for influence or model.

One can note that there is a near perfects ㄴ ㄷ ㄹ ㅁ ㅅ and Chinese ㄴ, ㄷ, 己, ㅁ, 人. The Chinese Zhùyīn Fúhào (中國語 注音符號) ㄷ [f] is also almost identical to the Korean ㄷ

[t]. Such matches are not surprising given that Chinese writing boasts more number of characters than any other writing system in the world.

We can turn to Japanese and find similar correspondences. We have the shape ヒ which originated from Korean 尼 [ni] and Japanese 比 [hi], respectively. On the other hand, ㅁ originated from the same 呂, but representing Korean (려[ryɔ]) and Japanese [ro], respectively. We also have Korean ㄱ from 야也[ya] and Japanese ユ from 由[yu].

But, for all the remarkable 'similarities' that one may find or observe between Hangeul and other writing systems, there are really no meaningful conclusions to be drawn from such observed similarities.

Because, for all the attested 'imitation' of writing systems to be found in the history of mankind, it would be a pointless attempt to search for a precedent or a model that King Sejong imitated in creating the Korean alphabet for the simple reason that his creation is the unique and unprecedented featural phonetic writing system in the world. There simply is nothing else like it in the world.

With this simple fact of uniqueness in the mind, all the previous scholarly attempts to find a model or a precedent for the Korean alphabet can be seen to have been a doomed venture from the start, just as such efforts by Ledyard and others (cf. 照那斯圖 2008) to find in 'Phags-pa a model for Hangeul, was doomed from the start to be pointless. This was despite his express agreement with the view that Hangeul was based on the shapes of the speech organs.

So, why are there still such attempts. Why haven't the scholars simply given recognition and credit where recognition and credit are due for uniqueness and ingeniousness. Envy has been humorously suggested as an explanation. But even if Hangeul is a justifiable object of envy, envy certainly should not be a foundation for scholarship.

The Korean alphabet, as an embodiment of King Sejong's genius, has offered the world a unique and unprecedented featural phonetic transcription system, the world's first 'Visible Speech' long before Bell's Visible Speech. It embodies 'graphical originality and ingenuity' worthy of praise and, dare I say, envy.

❖ References

An, Byeong-Hi(2007), *Hunminjeong-eum Yeon-gu*, Seoul : Seoul National University Press.

Coulmas, Florian(1989), *The Writing Systems of the World*. Cambridge, MA : Basil Blackwell Inc.

Coulmas, Florian(1996), *The Blackwell Encyclopedia of Writing Systems*. Oxford : Blackwell Inc.

Coulmas, Florian(2003), *Writing Systems : An Introduction to their Linguistic Analysis*.

Cambridge : Cambridge University Press.

Crystal, David(1987), *The Cambridge Encyclopedia of Language*, Cambridge : Cambridge University Press.

Daniels, Peter T. and William Bright, eds.(1996), *The World's Writing Systems.* Oxford : Oxford University Press

DeFrancis, John(1984), *The Chinese Language : Fact and Fantasy.* Honolulu : University of Hawai'i Press.

DeFrancis, John(1989), *Visible Speech : The Diverse Oneness of Writing Systems*, Honolulu : Univ. of Hawai'i Press.

Dürscheid, Christa(2006), *Einführung in die Schriftlinguistik*, Vandenhoeck & Ruprecht.

Février, James G.(1995), *Histoire de l'écriture, Payot & Rivages*,(2nd ed, 1959).

Fischer, Steven Roger(2001), *A History of Writing*, Reaktion Books.

Gelb, I. J.(1963), *A Study of Writing.* London,(2nd ed.)

Cheng, Ch'iao 鄭樵(1161), 六書略(Summary of six types of Chinese letters), 通志 Vol. 34, 元至治本(1935).

Junast 照那斯圖(2008), "The relationship between some basic letters in Hunminjeong-eum and 'Phags-pa script," in *the Proceedings of International Workshop on Hunminjeong-eum and 'Phags-pa script*, The Academy of Korean Studies.

Kang, Sin-Hang(1987), *Hunminjeong-eum Yeon-gu*, Rev. ed.(1990). Seoul : Sung Kyun Kwan University Press.

Kim, Chin-Woo(1997), "The structure of phonological units in Han'gul," in Young-Key Kim-Reanud, ed.(1997) 145-160.

Kim, Wanjin(1975), "Hunminjeong-eum jaumja-wa gahoek-euy wolli(The consonant letters in *Hunminjeong-eum* and the principle of adding strokes)," *Omunyeon'gu* 7-8, also in Lee Ki-Moon ed.(1977), 217-227.

Kim-Reanud, Young-Key ed.(1997), *The Korean Alphabet : Its History and Structure.* Honolulu : Univ. of Hawai'i Press.

King, Ross(1996), "Korean writing," in Peter T. Daniels & William Bright(1996) 218-227.

Ledyard, Gari K.(1966), The Korean language reform of 1446 : The origin, background and early history of the Korean alphabet. Ph.D. dissertation, University of California, Berkeley. Also in(1998), *The Korean Language Reform of 1446.* Seoul : Shingumunhwasa.

Ledyard, Gari K.(1997), "The international linguistic background of the Correct Sounds for the Instruction of the People," in Young-Key Kim-Renaud(1997) 31-87.

Lee, Ki-Moon ed.(1977), "Munja (Scripts)," *Gugeohak Nonmunseon* (Selected Papers in Korean Linguistics) 7, Seoul : Minjungseogwan.

Lee, Ki-Moon(1992), *Hunminjeong-eumchinjeron* (The evidences for none but King Sejong's invention of *Hunminjeong-eum*), *Hangukmunhwa* 13.

Lee, Sang-Oak(1997), "Graphical ingenuity in the Korean writing system : With new reference to calligraphy," in Young-Key Kim-Reanud, ed.(1997) 107-116.

Lee, Sang-Oak(2008), *Understanding Hunminjeong-eum*. Seoul : National Language Institute.

Lee, Sang-Oak(2009), "The Korean alphabet : An optimal featural system with graphical ingenuity," in Sang-Oak Lee, ed.(2009) 202-212.

Lee, Sang-Oak ed.(2009), *Written Language and Literacy*, Vol. 12, No. 2. Amsterdam : John Benjamins Publishing Co.

Rogers, Henry(2005), *Writing systems : A linguistic approach*. Malden, MA : Blackwell Publishing Co.

Sampson, Geoffrey(1985), *Writing systems*. Stanford, CA : Stanford University Press.

Sisayongosa ed.(1983), *The Korean Language*. Seoul : Sisayongosa.

Song, Ki Joong(2009), "'Phags-pa letters and Hunminjeong-eum," *Gugeohak*(*Korean Linguistics*) 54. 17-74.

Sproat, Richard(2000), *A Computational Theory of Writing Systems*, Cambridge : Cambridge University Press.

Taylor, Insup & M. Martin Taylor(1995), *Writing and Literacy in Chinese, Korean, and Japanese*. Amsterdam : John Benjamins Publishing Co.

web.meson.org/write/vs-overview.php

Wikipedia, History of the alphabet.

Yu, Chang-gyun(1966), "'Sanghyeong-i jabanggojeon'-e daehayeo (On the meaning of 'Symbolization and imitating the old letter style')," *Chindan hakpo* 29 & 30; also in Ki-Moon Lee, ed.(1977) 153-179.

✣ Appendix

Consonants   Vowels

𜵀 ka	𜵀 tta	𜵀 pa	𜵀 zha	𜵀 ha	𜵀 i
𜵀 kha	𜵀 ttha	𜵀 pha	𜵀 za	𜵀 'a	𜵀 u
𜵀 ga	𜵀 dda	𜵀 ba	𜵀 -a	𜵀 qa	𜵀 e
𜵀 nga	𜵀 nna	𜵀 ma	𜵀 ya	𜵀 xa	𜵀 o
𜵀 ca	𜵀 ta	𜵀 tsa	𜵀 ra	𜵀 fa	𜵀 ee
𜵀 cha	𜵀 tha	𜵀 tsha	𜵀 la	𜵀 gga	
𜵀 ja	𜵀 da	𜵀 dza	𜵀 sha		
𜵀 nya	𜵀 na	𜵀 wa	𜵀 sa		

Table 4

kä	a	(ra)	(qa)	ca	tsa	fa	pa	ta	ka
kwa	i	la	'a	cha	tsha	fha	pha	tha	kha
kya	u	ńźa	h	ja	dza	va	ba	da	ga
kra	e		ɣ	sha	sa	wa	ma	na	ng'a
rka	o		x	zha	za				
			y	nya					

Table 5

Western ←		→ Brahmic			→ Korean
Latin	Greek	Gujarati	Devanagari	Tibetan	
A	A	અ	अ	ཨ	
B	B	બ	ब	བ	ㅂ, ㅁ
C, G	Γ	ગ	ग	ག	ㄱ, (ㆁ)
D	Δ	ધ (ઢ)	ध (ढ)	-	
E	E	હ	ह	ཧ	(ㅸ)
F, V	F, Y	વ	व	ཝ	
Z	Z	૬ (s)	द (ड)	ད (ཌ)	ㄷ, ㄴ
H	H	ધ	घ	-	
-	Θ	થ (ઠ)	थ (ठ)	ཐ (ཋ)	
I, J	I	ય	य	ཡ	
K	K	ક	क	ཀ	
L	Λ	લ	ल	ལ	ㄹ
M	M	મ	म	མ	
N	N	ન	न	ན	
-	Ξ	શ	श	ཤ	
O	O	?			
P	Π	પ, ફ	प, फ	པ, ཕ	
-	ʔ	સ	स	ས	ㅈ, ㅅ
Q	Ọ	ખ	ख	ཁ	
R	P	ર	र	ར	
S	Σ	ષ	ष	ཥ	
T	T	ત (ઽ)	त (ट)	ཏ (ཊ)	

Table 6 : The spread of the alphabet west (Greek, Latin) and east (Brahmic, Korean).
(Cf, History of the alphabet from Wikipedia)

The Pictographic Map of Ten Traditional Symbols of Longevity

Sipjangsaeng (ten traditional Symbols of Longevity) corresponds to ten kinds of objects that symbolize immortality. Generally, they are regarded as the tortoise[龜], deer[鹿], crane[鶴], pine trees[松], bullocho(不老草) (elixir plants), mountains[山], water[水] or rivers[川], rocks[石], the sun[日], clouds[雲], or sometimes replaced by the moon[月], bamboo[竹] and peach[桃].

This picture is a 'munjado'(lit. graphic picture) drawn with letters. It is a work that only consists of pictographs which are published in the Jia Jin Zhuan Li Da Zi Dian 甲金篆隷大字典 (Sichuan Ci Shu Chu Ban She 四川辭書出版社, 1991). Since there is no one letter simply meaning *bullocho*, the sign of *bullo* (eternal youth) is taken note of by the green color of the canes.

This piece of art work is intended to help students who

study pictography to explore the meaning and function of symbols. Korean alphabets ㄱ-ㅂ are included inside the ㅁ or ㅂ of the word 石 (ㅂ can be seen in the variant of seal script of 石), trying to show the intrinsic order in which the shapes of characters are expanded by adding strokes. Also, an email address, which makes interactions between the artist and the appreciators possible, is written at the place of 'Nakgwan' (落款) like a signature, trying to introduce the information technique of the new era into paintings for the first time.

sangoak2@gmail.com / www.sangoak.com

The Pictographic Map of Zoo

In the Jia Jin Zhuan Li Da Zi Dian (Sichuan Ci Shu Chu Ban She, 1991), the Chinese oracle bone and seal scripts have reflected the several thousand years of amusing work in pictorialization, especially related to animals. Due to the process of abstraction of animal shapes, it is convincing to claim that Chinese characters, either in the field of orthography or art, are much more rational than pictographs of any other regions in the world.

More than 240 characters out of the Chinese pictographs have been chosen to show in this zoo munjado (character picture). Many different interesting characters being placed, the interior of the zoo becomes very complicated. Therefore, the tortoise, deer and crane of Sipjangsaeng are left out. Cow [牛], horse [馬], sheep [羊], pig [豬], dog [犬], cat [貓], fox [狐], wolf

[狼], ape [猿], bear [熊], rang (a type of ape)[獇], tiger [虎], lion [獅子], leopard [豹], wildcat [狸], camel [駱駝], elephant [象], kylin [麒麟], rhinoceros [犀], hippo [河馬], etc. are included in the munjado. Also, the twelve Earthly Branches: Zi (rat), Chou (cow), Yin (tiger), Mao (rabbit), Chen (dragon), Si (snake), Wu (horse), Wei (sheep), Shen (monkey), You (rooster), Xu (dog) and Hai (pig); fishes: carp, shark, whale and crocodile; birds: crow, duck, dove, sparrow, peacock, wild goose, eagle, goose and chick; imaginative birds: roc, phoenix (specially incorporated into this zoo, though it is, the same as dragon, not an existent animal) can be seen. There is also a zebra with black and white bands hiding under the giraffe.

At each joint of the zigzag, ㅊ which includes ㅅ and ㅈ, or ㅋ, ㅌ, ㅍ can be seen. Also, Korean alphabets ㅅ-ㅎ including ㅇ, ㅎ are shown to represent the intrinsic order of the consonant shapes. The pronunciation or the shape of the word 之 is similar to z, so it accounts for the first letter of the word 'zoo'. The picture is divided by the shape of the word ZOO into different sections. Except the sky, each can be referred as the different categorized fence, pen or partition of a zoo. Also, the email at the place of 'Nakgwan' (signature) and the Hong Kong New Year decoration besides the rabbit are grafted onto the picture.

sangoak@snu.ac.kr

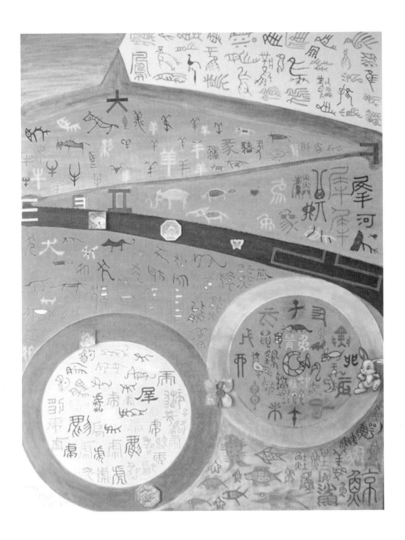

The Map of Pictographic Origins
and Sign Systems

On the world map as follows, which illustrates the places of origin of proto-letters, the location of Korea is creatively designated by a Korean alphabet. It is shown that the Korean vowels are organized into a radiating shape, and the writing in digital form is more favorable than Roman letters.

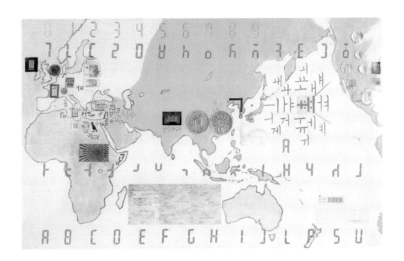

Looking at the world's origin of pictographs from the perspective of orthography of linguistics, Mesopotamia and East Mediterranean Sea regions, Egypt, India, China, Maya (Mexico and so on) are considered as places of civilization. Even though the latter letters were originated from them, the shapes of those letters lost pictorial components because the pictographic flavor waned. Among the letters, the pictographic flavor is widely found in the Chinese characters, particularly in seal scripts or epigraphs. This feature even becomes an element of painting. In Korean consonants, ㄱ, Δ, o are drawn in the same way as in other regions on the earth. Korean vowels took the shapes of the heaven, earth and man, and were extended to 21 characters through different combination of these basic elements. These common bases are integrated into the blue rectangle at the center.

Dots(점) can be connected both vertically and horizontally to form characters. Numbers, Korean consonants and English letters are written in the digital form of 日. Numbers are drawn on the earth's longitude to mark the time zone. For Korean alphabets, 14 of them can all be shown, though there somehow need changes of the shapes. However, it is difficult to present all the English letters K, M, N, O (to be equal to D), Q, R, T, V, W, X, Y, Z. As for English, 14 letters can be shown while the other 12 cannot.

Bar codes and QR codes are the wider modern sign systems. The 12 Chinese zodiac animals on the chocolate wrapper and their pictographs are placed to where China is on the map. Apart from this, chocolate wrappers in copper coin and liquor bottle label design, which contains characters, are stuck onto the corresponding areas. Under the Indian Ocean, the space is filled with an art work by Kim Sungsil. The composition of this map is enriched by using other materials on hand.

For South America, pictographs did not exist, so characters that appeared in the Mayan civilization of North America were the only letters.

www.sangoak.com

我對文字略有研究，特別是中國文字。象形文字本身就是一種藝術，我認爲中國人要爲象形文字的發明感到驕傲。懇請您欣賞我以下的二个作品：

十长生文字图 (图一)

韩国的十长生是指象征长寿的十种物象，包括龟、鹿、鹤、松、不老草、山、水、石、日、云。此外，川、月、竹、桃等也可与上述十种物象互相替换。这幅文字图以记载于甲金篆隶大字典(四川辞书出版社，1991)的象形文字构成。因为没有一个单独的象形文字代表「不老草」，所以作家藉由绿色的竹来标志「不老」。这画作旨在帮助研究象形文字的学生探究符号象征的意味及作用。在「石」字的「ㅁ」和「ㅂ」形状中(ㅂ可见于「石」的篆字异形)，我们可观察到韩语的声母「ㄱ-ㅂ」。这构图目的在于表现以加添笔画来扩展字型的内在跌序(내재질서)。此外，作家初次尝试把新世代的科技注入绘画中－－以电邮地址作为落款，让观赏者能以电邮方式与作家沟通。

动物园文字图 (图二)

在甲金篆隶大字典(四川辞书出版社，1991)中，甲骨文及篆书反映了中国数千年来有趣的象形化作业，尤其与动物相关的。基于动物形状的抽象化过程，不论在语言学或艺术的层面上，都让人信服汉字比世界上任何地方的象形文字更合乎理性。

作家选了超过240个文字表现在这幅动物园文字图中。因为很多不同有趣的字型令动物园里头变得十分夏杂，所以十长生的龟、鹿和鹤被除去。文字图中包括牛、马、羊、猪、犬、猫、狐、狼、猿、熊、獾、虎、狮子、豹、狸、骆驼、象、麒麟(长颈鹿)、犀、河马等。图中还可见十二支：子(鼠)、丑、寅、卯(兔)、辰(龙)、巳(蛇)、午、未、申、酉(鸡)、戌和亥；鱼类：鲤、沙鱼、鲸和鳄鱼；鸟类：乌鸦、鸭、鸠(鸽)、麻雀、孔雀、雁、鹰、鹅和雏；假想鸟类：鹏和凤(虽然与龙一样不是真实存在的动物，但在这里作特别编入)。在长颈鹿下方，更藏着一只拥有黑白间纹的斑马。

在每个「之」字形的连接点，我们可以看见包含「ㅅ」和「ㅈ」的「ㅊ」、「ㅋ」、「ㅌ」或「ㅍ」。此外，图中包含「ㅇ」和「ㅎ」的韩语文字「ㅅ－ㅎ」代表着韩语声母的内在跌序(내재질서)。「之」字的发音和形状都跟「Z」很相似，所以作家以其代表英文词「ZOO」的第一个字母「Z」。这幅动物园文字图的结构被「ZOO」的字型分成不同区域。除了天空的部份，各区域可被视作动物园里以围栏作不同分类的区隔。此外，以电邮地址作为落款的手法及处于兔子旁的香港新年装饰物被融合于作品中。

www.sangoak.com의 연구실적에 추가할 사항

저서/*편저

1981 *Metrical phonology* Ⅰ, Ⅱ, Seoul : Han Shin Moon Hwa Sa, Ⅰ
 p.88, Ⅱ p.343.

1999 『(외국인을 위한) 한국어 교육의 방법과 실제』, 서울 : 한국방송
 대학교출판부, xv, p.623 <남기심, 홍재성과 공저>

2003 Kore dili / İ İk.sop, İ Sang.ok, Çae Van ; çev. Sultan Ferah
 Akpınar, Baski : Aydogdu, x iii , p.478 (한국의 언어, 터키어판)
 <이익섭, 채완과 공저>

2008 『韓國語槪論』(=한국의 언어; 張光軍, 江波 譯 Zhang, Guangjun;
 Jiang, Bo) 世界圖書出版公司北京公司, p.310 <李翊燮, 李相億, 蔡琬
 著>

2008 *You Can Learn the Korean Alphabet in One Morning*, 서울 : 소통,
 p.100.

2008 『한국어와 한국문화』(영어판), Korean Language and Culture, 서
 울 : 소통, p.480, 2011 개정 2판.

2008 『<알기 쉽게 풀어 쓴> 훈민정음』(Утгыг тайлж хялбаршуул
 сан) Хунмин жонгым, 국립국어원 편, p.160 (권말에 '훈민정음
 해례본, 언해본' 영인본 수록, 한국어-몽골어 대역본, 번역 : 성비
 락, 교정 : 델렉냠 엥호자야) <강신항 · 김주원과 공저>

2008 『<알기 쉽게 풀어 쓴> 훈민정음』(Tim hieu noi dung cua) Huan
 Dàn Chinh Âm 국립국어원 편, p.156, [94] (부록 : 영인 『훈민정
 음』 해례본, 언해본, 베트남어 교정 : 꾸억바오, 번역 : 다우티미
 칸) <강신항 · 김주원과 공저>

2010 *Contemporary Korean Linguistics : International Perspectives*,
 Kyǒnggi- do P'aju-si : Taehaksa, 2010. xii, p.414 ; Also other
 co-edition : in honor of professor Sang-Oak Lee / edited by

디자이너 세종의 독창성

Robert J. Fouser, xvi, p.423.

2012 *Korean Through English, New Edition* (1st Edition in 1992, 2nd in 1998) Book One, Seoul : Hollym, p.184. <이승미와 공저>

2013 *Korean Through English, New Edition* (1st Edition in 1992, 2nd in 1998) Book Two, Seoul : Hollym, p.232. <정영미와 공저>

2013 『한국어와 한국문화』(일어판), 韓國語と韓國文化, 서울 : 소통, p.446.

2014 『한국어와 한국문화』(중어판), 韓國語及韓國文化, 서울 : 소통, p.436.

2014 『역대 한국어 형태 사전』, 서울 : 서울대 출판부(예정).

2014 『디자이너 세종의 독창성 : 한글의 숨은 코드』, 서울 : 역락(예정)

논문

2009 "The Korean Alphabet : An Optimal Featural System with Graphical Ingenuity," *Written Language and Literacy* 12.2, Amsterdam : John Benjamin, 202-212.(Special Issue : Writing Systems and Linguistic Structure, Guest Editor : Sang-Oak Lee)

2010 "Contrastive Phonology between Cantonese, Hakka and Sino-Korean, and between Cantonese and Sino-Japanese," in *Contemporary Korean Linguistics : International Perspectives*, (ed. by Sang-Oak Lee), Kyŏnggi-do P'aju-si : Taehaksa, 385-414.

2011 "Not Copy but Envy : The Korean Alphabet Did not Imitate Mongol 'Phags-pa but Was Invented with Graphical Originality," *Inquiries into Korean Linguistics IV*, Kyŏnggi-do P'aju-si : Taehaksa, 143-164. (ed. by James H.-S. Yoon et al.)

2014 "Proverbial homogeneity : A cross-linguistic examination of Korean and Indonesian : With reference to English and Chinese proverbs," *Korean Linguistics 16.1*, Amsterdam : John Benjamin, 63-81.

기고

1979   촘스키의 언어 혁명,『월간 독서』79. 4.

1980   위험한 사고,『대우가족』66호 80.1.

1980   시험 당하는 인생,『대우가족』67호 80.2.

1980   옥상 채소밭,『대우가족』70호 80.5.

1989   '하늘'과 '아가리',『조선일보』8/17. '一事一言'에 게재.

1989   음성합성과 음성인식,『조선일보』8/24. '一事一言'에 게재.

1989   독을 뺀 전갈,『조선일보』8/30. '一事一言'에 게재.

1991   위성통신강의와 국제학술교류 : 1.배경 2. 편성 및 내용 3. 활용
        도 4. 기자재, (서울대학교)『대학신문』11/18, 1316호 p.4.

1996   곡구(曲球)를 하는 이유,『호주동아』96.10

1997   로마자 표기법은 사용자 위주로, 사회발전연구소,『한국인』
        16.7 : 108 - 111.

1999   무공해 캠퍼스,『대학신문』9/20, 1506호 p.3.

2002   '우리'들의 대한민국-한국학의 미래와 지향,『대학신문』9/9,
        1584호 p.7.

2008   한글은 말이 아니라 글,『LA중앙일보』10/08, 미주판 p.20.

2008   독도가 외롭지 않게 하려면,『LA중앙일보』10/29, 미주판 p.17.

2008   'BMW'를 타야하는 이유 : Bus, Metro, Walking,『LA중앙일보』
        12/20, 미주판 p.18.

2009   '명당' 코리아 타운 가꾸기,『LA중앙일보』1/13, 미주판 p.19.

2009   서울대 역사에 기록해야 할 '이 땅 최초의' 일들,『서울대학교
        명예교수 회보』5 : 136-142.

2010   한인타운에 홍살문을 세우자 [코리아타운 지키기 특별 제안]『아
        크로폴리스』2/11, (LA 서울대 동창회 사이트) AcropolisTimes.
        com

2010   아크로 곁에 있으니 '아침이슬'이 절로. [창간 1주년 특별기고]
        『아크로폴리스』3/22.

2011   유럽 변방과 모로코 여행,『서울대학교 명예교수 회보』7 :
        158-164.

2012   트위트를 스위트하고 스마트하게 쓰자, <굿소사이어티>(사이
        트) 2/22.

2013   음악(音惡), 미술 (迷術) 그리고 문학(文虐),『굿소사이어티』2/25,

『경기 Kyunggi 59회보』 52호, 10-11.

2013 세 가지 미스터리 : 초상화가, 월문 소재, 채색 석탑,『박물관 뉴스』 505호, 22-23.

2013 룩소르 신전의 사과 한 알―이스라엘/요르단/이집트 기행문, 서울대학교 명예교수회보 9 : 158-164.

2013 진실본과 조작본 또는 사실과 허위, <www.sangoak.com> 게시판 10/21.

2014 (최고 존엄 초상화) 방패 막이 및 문제점 (원전) 인근 거주조치, <www.sangoak.com> 게시판 1/11.

부 록

언어/문자 관련 작품
[문자만 관련되는 작품에는 #표]

- 양말(兩말²)
- 다리 읽기
- # 江水三千里
- 가창(*佳唱)오리
- 팔괘도(八卦圖) −십이지(十二支) −이십사절기(二十四節氣)−
  Zodiac − 十二支二十四氣節圖
- 이집트 여행 기념작
- # 몽고문자 臨書, 첩해몽어 제1권 4
- # 상형문자 호리병 : 이집트 문자 + 한자 전서(篆書)
- # 이상억(Sang Oak Lee) 첫 자 문장(initial 紋章)
- 동북공정도(東北攻征圖)
- 필천벌 불회자(必天罰 不悔者)
- # 송북 종북좌파(送北 從北左派)---독수리 삼형제 중 1
- 난지행(亂芝行)
- 잡스의 미발표 작품은 iDiot?
  [2012년 1월 5일 조선일보 오피니언] 이상억 기고문

2014년 말띠해 기념작, 말과 양말(내면 구조)

*2015년이 되면 그림 속에 양(羊)이 추가될 예정임.

양말(兩말²)

Q : 이것이 뭐예요?

A : 말입니다.

B : 아니에요.

A : 그럼 양말(洋襪)입니다.

B : 그것도 아니에요.

A : 그럼, 양(兩)-말, 즉 두 말입니다.

B : 글쎄요. 양말을 보고 말이라고 하세요? 참!

A : 그렇다면 이것은 말도 양말도 아니군요.

　　그러나 눈앞에 뭔가 있으니, 말과 양말이 동시에 보인다고

　　해야 맞겠습니다.

다리 읽기*

다리(脚)인지 다리(橋)인지,
아니면 다리의 다리(橋脚)인가?
그야말로 양다리 걸친 말이구나!

*정월 대보름에 '다리 밟기'를 하면 1년간 다리가 아프지 않는다고 한다. 서울
광교와 수표교의 다리 밟기 풍경을 최남선은 이렇게 적고 있다.
'…장안의 남녀들이 종가로 모여들어 보신각의 저녁 종소리를 듣고 나서 각
곳에 있는 다리로 흩어져 가서 밤새도록 다리 위를 왔다 갔다 하였다. 서로를
어깨와 다리가 부딪힐 정도로 붐비면서 날나리와 장고를 울리고 시를 읊기도
하며 물에 비친 달을 보며 1년 동안에 좋은 일이 있길 빌었다.'
맨 위 장면과도 맞는 흥겨운 세시풍습으로 답교놀이[踏橋戲]라고도 한다.

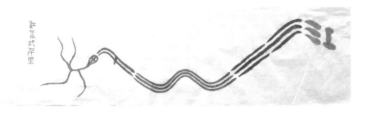

江水三千里

'江水三千里'라는 글자를 써서 실제 중국의 양자강 모양처럼 상해 지역부터 [江 자의 시작에 上 모양이 상해 위치] 중경 지역까지 강이 왼쪽으로 흐르는 주류를 그려 본 셈이다. '江水三千里'라는 말은 원래 明나라 袁凱의 京師得家書詩에서 "江水三千里,-----, 只道早還鄕"라고 읊은 데서 따온 것이다. 양자강은 삼천리의 먼 거리를 흐른다는 뜻으로, 여행 중 멀리 있는 자기 집을 생각하며 그리워하는 데 쓰는 고사성어다.

揚子江 flows 三千里 which is long distance for travelers to long for their home. From 明 袁凱's 京師得家書詩 : 江水三千里,-----,只道早還鄕.

江水三千里 is written in the actual shape of 揚子江. Please enjoy these pictographic picture.

가창(*佳唱)오리

너희들은 왜 그 신비로운 소리를 내며 그리 멋있게 나니?
이십만 날개 짓 합친 소리로 可唱오리?

*가창은 순우리말로 한자가 없다. 서산 간척지나 주남 저수지 등에
한때 20만 마리씩 떼지어 나타날 때는 아침 저녁 두 번 신비로운
소리를 내며 날았다. 날아오르고 또 돌아와 내리는 소리가 아름다
워 가히 佳唱이라 할 만하고, 可唱의 오리라 할 만도 하다.

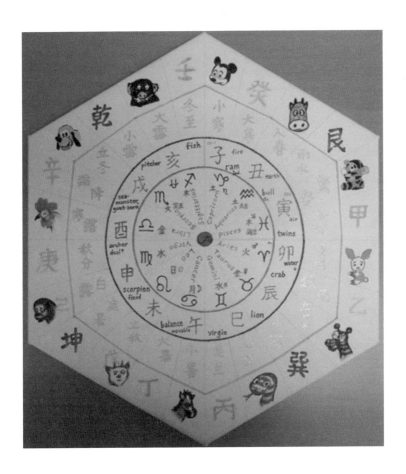

팔괘도(八卦圖)−십이지(十二支)−이십사절기(二十四節氣)
−Zodiac

한가운데 태극을 두었는데, 이 모양을 국기 중앙에 둔 한국은
북쪽에 붉은색을 좋아하는 공산국가, 남쪽에 푸른색을 좋아하는
민주국가가 대치하고 있는 형상이 우연히 일치한다. 태극을 양
분하는 곡선은 현재 DMZ의 모습과도 흡사하다. 그 태극 둘레의

영문은 zodiac이고, 그 더 밖의 기호들도 서양의 12지에 해당하는 상징들(Leo사자 등)이다. 그 한 둘레 더 밖에 동양의 12지에 해당하는 한자들(子=쥐 등)을 zodiac의 명칭들과 함께 보였다. 다음 노란색 둘레에 써 놓은 한자가 24절기 이름이다. 맨 가장자리의 그림들은 12지에 해당하는 동물들이고, 그 사이사이에 십간과 4괘의 글자들을 써 넣었다.

In this picture, the *taegeuk* symbol is placed at the center. The South Korean national flag also has this symbol placed at the center. The design of the taegeuk symbol happens to coincide with the situation in Korea, the North which is a communist country prefers red and the South which is a democratic country prefers blue. The curved line which divides the *taegeuk* symbol into two is like the present DMZ. The English words around the taegeuk is zodiac, while the circle outer includes western symbols of the zodiac. The next outer one shows the Chinese characters and English names of the Eastern ziodiac. Names of the 24 solar terms are written within the yellow circle. At the very edge, the animals, between which are Chinese characters of the Ten Heavenly Stems and four trigrams, correspond to the ziodiac.

十二支二十四气节图

在图三，太极被放于正中间。韩国把太极图案置于国旗的中央，而这图案的模样恰巧与南北对峙的情况一致－－北方是共产国家，偏好红色；南方是民主国家，偏好蓝色。把太极一分为二的曲线，就如当今的韩半岛非武装地带(DMZ)。太极的周围是十二星座的英文；再下一个圈是象征十二支的西方符号(如狮子)；再下一个圈是东方十二支的汉字(如子)及黄道十二宫的名称。黄色圈中的汉字是二十四节气的名字。最边缘的图案是与十二支相对应的动物。动物图中间所写的汉字是十干及四卦。

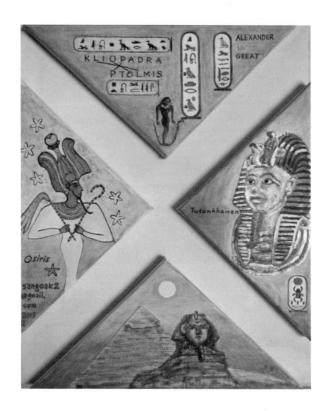

이집트 여행 기념작(시계 방향으로 설명)

－프랑스 어학자 상폴리옹이 주목했던 L, O, P자의 일치를 시작으로 상형문자를 해독하게 되었음. 알렉산더, 클레오파트라, 프톨레미스 등의 고유명사는 타원속에.

－투탄카멘 왕의 장례 가면. 밑에는 왕의 비석 둘레에 새긴 타원형 문장의 상형자.

－스핑크스와 카프르 왕의 피라밋. 스핑크스의 얼굴은 복원된 모습으로 그림.

－지팡이와 노리깨를 든 오시리스 신. 지하세계로부터 생명을 부여하는 힘을 가진 신.

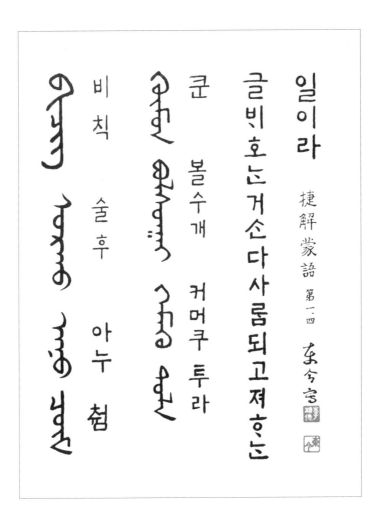

몽고문자 臨書, 첩해몽어 제1권 4

서예 작품으로 몽골어를 쓴 최초의 시도는 1969년이었다.

소위 알타이 어족이라는 몽골, 만주, 일본 (터키는 멀어서 그 주변에) 모두 침략을 해와 역서(譯書)가 필요했던 것이다.

\# 상형문자 호리병 : 이집트 문자 + 한자 전서(篆書)

Sang Oak Lee '96

이상억(Sang Oak Lee) 첫 자 문장(initial 紋章)

시드니에서 배운 작업(1996)

동북공정도(東北攻征圖)

아다시피 동북공정(東北工程)은 억지로 만든 역사 문제이지만, 우선 황사와 미세먼지(PM10), 초미세먼지(PM2.5) 등의 스모그, 조류독감(AI)까지 날아오고, 불법 어로가 자행되는 실제 상황에서 현실적 공정(攻征)문제가 더 다급하다. 뿐만 아니라 최근의 항공 구역 및 영해 확장, 중국 자본의 진출 등도 잘 조정해야 할 당면 문제들이다.

그러나 중국은 몽고와 만주족의 침략을 빼고는, 고래로 한반도에 문화적 수준을 높여주는 입력을 많이 해 왔다. 그에 비해 다음에 말할 일본은 야요이 시대에 한반도에서 도래인이 와 벼 농사를, 백제 멸망 후 유민이 축성술을, 조선에서 납치되어 온 도공이 백자 기술을 가르치는 등, 수많은 은혜를 받고도; 삼국시 대엔 해적들이 칼로, 임진왜란 땐 조총으로, 식민통치 때는 남자 의 노동과 목숨, 여자의 정조와 또 곡물을 수탈하는 폐만 끼쳤다.

그 동안 모든 한일간 이슈가 한국에 대해 공세적으로 피해를 주어온 것들이고, 해결이 된다 해도 한국은 원상 복귀를 하기(본 전 찾기)도 다 어려운 경우들이다. 그러나 진정한 반성과 합당한 변상을 하지 않고도 일본은 계속 한국이 어렵게 한다고 트집을 잡는다. 입장을 바꿔 일본이 그렇게 당했다면 어찌 해 왔을까?

뭐, 야스쿠니 신사 전범 합장 문제만 해도, 공연히 그런 장소 와 문제거리를 설정해 놓고 이웃 나라 비위 긁는 데 쓰는 간교 한 천박성이 일부 일본인의 본성이다. 설사 그런 신사를 참배하 는 문제가 안 일어난다 해도 한국이나 중국이 실제 얻는 것은 명분 외에는 별로 없다. 일본은 보상을 더 하지 않고도 문제를 다른 곳에 묶어두는 방법으로 신사 문턱을 드나든다.

중국이 안중근 의사 기념관을 만든 일도 일본을 약오르게 하 는 전략이었듯이, 한국도 독도를 달라는 일본에 대마도를 내놓 으라고 적극 공세로 나가는 전략을 써 봄직하다. 세종대왕이 정 복했던 땅이었으니까.

임진왜란을 일으킨 일본인에게 조선통신사는 문화와 평화를 가르쳤다. 이는 정권이 호전적이었더라도 일반 국민은 다 그렇 지 않았을 때 호감이 살아나는 것이다. 그런데 지금 일본인들은?

필천벌 불회자(必天罰 不悔者)

　원래 일본 신도 사원 앞의 도리이(鳥居) 모양이 丹자 비슷하다. 天자는 애초에는 써넣지 않았으나 신사 문 기둥과 비슷한 모양으로 그들의 神도 벌을 줄 것이란 의미로 그려 넣었다. 그 옆의 욱일승천기(旭日昇天旗)는 군국주의 기치 아래 흘린 피를 상징하는데 제격이다. 바다 속에서 일어난 지진은 쓰나미를 몰고 일본 동해안을 덮치며, 화산에서 솟아나온 용암은 열도를 붉게 덮는다. 이 물로 Mitsubishi 중공업과 Aso 가문의 (赤坂)탄광 등에서 저지른 강제 노동의 죄가 씻기고, 이 불로 성노예로서 강제 당했던 여성의 혼이 위안 받기를 기원한다.

　부디 죄수번호 #731 Abe, learn real RIGHT (正, 右) from

Germany! 정말 바른 길이 무엇이고, 진정한 우익의 사상과 행동이 어찌해야 하는 것인지 생각 좀 해 보기 바란다. 그리고 아무리 떼를 써도 애초부터 독도는 한국 땅이다.

모든 이슈가 한국에 대해 공세적으로 피해를 주는 것들이었고 또 사실은, 일본 땅에서조차 관동대지진 때 한국인 학살이나 현재 혐한 시위에서 위협적 작태로 인종 학대를 일삼고 있다. 일본인들은 잘못을 인정하면 하라키리를 해서 배를 갈라야 하니까 웬만해선 잘못했다고 못한다는데, 그러지 않고도 현대 독일인들처럼 쿨하게 반성하고 진심으로 보상적 행동을 하는 방향도 있음을 배워야 한다.

한국과 가까이 있지 않다면 국민성이 어떤들 큰 상관이 없겠지만 바로 옆에서 이렇게 폐를 끼치는 일본이 있음은 불행이다.

송북 종북좌파(送北 從北左派)---독수리 삼형제 중 1*

독수리가 물고 가는 사람 모양의 것은, 10시 방향으로 고개를 갸우뚱해 보면, 이 사람이 左派라고 左자가 쓰여 있다. 좌파 모두를 지칭하는 것이 아니라 "종북을 부르짖는" 좌파들만 독수리가 골라 그들이 염원하는 북한으로 보내 준다는 그림이다.

*독수리 오형제가 아니라 삼형제만 그렸는데, 다른 두 그림 중 하나는 다음에 보이겠으나, 또 더 하나 '天池獄 投下 : 북한 희화'는 언어/문자와는 약한 관련만 있어 여기 싣지 아니 하였다.

난지행(亂芝行)

　蘭芝島의 옛이름에는 亂자를 썼기 때문에 亂芝行이라고 題함. 어쨌든 '부뚜막의 난지도행'으로, 밑 왼쪽은 여의도 쌍둥이 빌딩, 오른쪽은 옛 쓰레기섬 난지도의 요즘 모습.

　-2012년 4월 총선전 작품. 임진왜란 이후 420년이 되었으나 "정치 청소"가 필요한 사정은 변치 않아 많은 이가 동의하였고, 이와 비슷한 만평이 같은 해 한 달 뒤 중앙일보에도 실렸다.

잡스의 미발표 작품은 iDiot?

스마트해지려면 생각을 해야지.

2012년 1월 5일 조선일보 오피니언에 이상억 기고문
[국문을 영역해 뒤에 붙임]

© Sang Oak Lee 2012

스티브 잡스는 2011년을 뜨겁게 달구며 불같이 살다 갔다. 이 해를 접는 시점에서 추모 열기 후에 냉철히 성찰할 필요도 있다. Apple, iMac은 물론 iPod, iPhone, iPad, iTunes, iOs, iCloud, iBooks, iMovie, iPhoto, iWeb, iDVD, iLife, iWork라는 수많은 Hardware와 Software에 걸쳐 i 시리즈를 만들어 놓았다. 아울러 수많은 Apps를 개발 유도해 활용할 수 있게 했다. 웬만한 일을 스마트폰 하나에서 할 수 있도록 기능화 해놓았으니 무척 편리해진 것이다. 약속시간에 늦어도 쉽게 연락할 수 있는 핸드폰이 여행 중 도로나 맛집 찾기에도 쉬운 스마트폰이 되었다. 이메일도 움직이면서 아무 곳에서나 응대할 수 있다.

Steve Jobs left us in 2011, leaving us with a glorious trail of innovations, to the last. As we turn over to a new year, having finished the year memorializing Steve Jobs, perhaps we should start the new year with some reflection. Aside from Apple and iMac, Steve Jobs left us with numerous innovations in both hardware and software as iPad, iPhone, iPad, iTunes, iOs, iCloud, iBooks, iMovie, iPhoto, iWeb, iDVD, iLife, and iWorks. Such works have made our lives that much more convenient, as many of our works can pretty much be handled by a smart phone. We can not only make calls on the road if we are running late to an appointment but also while we are traveling, we can eeily locate the roads and restaurants, all with a few fingering on a smartphone. Anywhere, any time, we can also just as easily receive and send emails.

요즘 많은 사람들이 길거리나 차 안에서 한 손을 올려 손전화기를 잡고 있는 형상이다. 주변에 주의를 못 주다가 교통사고를 당하기도 하고, 운전 시에도 어물거리는 형색이 드러난다. 이 정도의 부작용은 주의를 하면 피할 수 있다. 그러나 사실은 보편적으로 더 큰 문제가 일어나고 있다. 편리한 Apps를 보고 스마트하게 사는 것 같지만 그것을 찾아 단순히 이용하는 데는 능해도, 좀더 심층적 사고를 해서 새로운 아이디어를 낸다든지 하는 일에는 둔해진다. 손끝으로 조작은 잘 해도 머리를 써서 생각할 시간과 기회가 없기 때문이다. 과잉된 정보의 노예로 헤어나지 못하는 현상이 도처에 일어나고 있다. '잡스'러운 Apps도 있어서 차라리 없어야 좋겠다는 생각이 드는 것도 있다.

　　We often see drivers on the road with one hand holding their phone. Unable to pay full attention to their driving, accidents are the natural consequences. Such drivers also move hesitantly over the roads. While such problems can be avoided if the drivers simply pay more attention to their driving, we are in fact faced with a broader and bigger problem : We may appear to be "living smarter" with the help of the convenient Apps. But, in truth, while we have become more "capable" in simply finding and using such Apps, we are becoming increasingly "less capable" in actually coming up with new ideas and engaging in extended meditations. We are increasingly allocating much of our time to flickering and gesturing with our fingers, and less of our time to thinking with our head. Everywhere, we find we are becoming slaves to the flood of information. For all the conveniences of Job's Apps, one cannot wonder if we might not be better off without them.

원래 우리 생활은 남과 관계 속에서 하는 부분과 나 자체 속에서 하는 부분이 적절히 조화를 이루어야 한다. 하루 중 많은 시간을 스마트 폰이나 iPad를 붙들고 있는데 쓰면, 대인 관계나 정보 입수에는 유리해질지 몰라도 자신이 창작할 값진 내용은 쌓이지 못한다. 가령 음악가나 소설가가 집중해야 할 시간에 스마트폰이 울리고 그 응대에 긴 시간을 쓰게 된다면 결코 좋은 연주나 작품은 나올 수 없겠다. 현대인은 의문의 갈증 속에 생각하고 고민하고 연구하고 판단할 시간이 적다. 이렇게 되면 결국 스마트해지기는 어렵다. 오랫동안 이런 악순환이 쌓이면 결국 i 시리즈를 쓴 결과 iDiot(아이디어트)라는 인간 신제품이 양산될 것이다. 이것이 잡스도 모르는 사이에 예비해 놓은 미발표 작품이었다면 우리는 이제라도 깊이 생각을 좀 해 봐야겠다. 잡스도 인간들이 스마트 기기로 인해 '아이디어트=이디어트'가 되는 것을 바라지는 않았을 것이다. 잡스가 외친 Stay foolish!의 진의는 '바보로 남아라'가 아니다. 항상 우직하게 생각하고 탐구해서 스마트해지도록 잘난 척하지 말란 뜻일 것이다. 남이 정리해 놓은 Apps만 따라다니는 데 시간을 다 쏟고 독창적인 사고를 못하는 인간이 어찌 제2의 잡스가 될 수 있겠는가?

In truth, our lives should harmonize and balance "our relationship with others" and "our relationship with ourselves." While the many hours we give over to smart phones may prove useful in our information gathering and in our personal relationships, these are the same valuable hours that are definitely lost to creativity. If our writers and musicians are devoting most of their day to making and answering calls, or fingering through their apps, how can we expect inspiring books or moving music. Our modern lives and smart phones appear to be robbing us of time to muse, to think, to explore, and to doubt deeply. If we live our lives like this, how can we hope for our lives to be truly SMART? Indeed, if we go on spending much of our day with i-series, we may have no choice but to end up as just another i-product, an unintended but unavoidable iDiot. There is no doubt that Steve Jobs never intended for his i-products to produce an idiot. We have to keep in mind that when Steve Jobs asked us to "Stay foolish!" he didn't mean for us to "Stay a fool" but for us to stay innocent, to stay venturesome, and to stay modest as we make a way to wisdom and to smartdom. If we spend too much of our time with the Apps, to the point that we have no time to give to our own thoughts and to our own originality, how can we hope for another Steve Jobs.

이상억 李相億

(現 서울大學校 國語國文學科 名譽敎授) www.sangoak.com

1969-1973	서울大學校 文理科大學 및 大學院 國語國文學科 文學士, 碩士取得, 博士課程修了, 同 語學硏究所 外國人韓國語課程 助敎 및 講師
1973-1978	Fulbright Scholar로 美國 University of Illinois at Urbana 大學院 言語學科, 言語學碩士, 博士
1975-1977	美國 Havard-Yenching Institute, Research Fellow (客員硏究員)
1980-1981	濠洲 Australian National University 招聘敎授
1982-2009	서울大學校 人文大學 國語國文學科 敎授
1985-1986	독일 Humboldt 財團招請 München 및 Bochum 大學 硏究敎授
1987-1989	서울大學校-UCLA 韓國內 韓國語文化敎育 課程責任者
1987-1989	서울大學校 敎務副處長
1990-1994	서울大學校-UCLA 및 호주 Griffith대와 Telelink(인터넷)敎育 課程 責任者
1994-1997	호주 University of Sydney 韓國學 擔當招聘敎授
1996	第3次 PACKS 大會(호주 시드니大) 組織委員長
2002-2004	國際韓國言語學會(ICKL) 會長
2006-2008	서울大學校 人文學硏究院 韓國語硏究所所長
2006	55回 서울市 文化賞 人文科學部分 受賞
2008-2009	서울大學校 美洲센터 設立團長兼 UCLA韓國學 講義 敎授

디자이너 세종의 독창성 : 한글의 숨은 코드
Ingenious Designer Sejong : the Hidden Code in Designing Hangeul

초판 인쇄 2014년 9월 24일 | **초판 발행** 2014년 10월 2일
지은이 이상억
펴낸이 이대현
편 집 박선주 | **디자인** 이홍주
펴낸곳 도서출판 역락 | **등록** 제303-2002-000014호(등록일 1999년 4월 19일)
주 소 서울시 서초구 동광로 46길 6-6
전 화 02-3409-2058, 2060 | **팩시밀리** 02-3409-2059 | **전자우편** youkrack@hanmail.net
ISBN 979-11-5686-084-6 03710

정가 12,000원

* 파본은 책은 구입처에서 교환해 드립니다

이 도서의 국립중앙도서관 출판예정 도서목록(CIP)은 서지정보 유통지원 시스템 홈페이지(http://seoji.nl.go.kr)와 국가자료 공동목록 시스템(http://www.nl.go.kr/kolisnet)에서 이용하실 수 있습니다. (CIP제어번호 : CIP2014026529)